Instant Bible Lessons

Virtues and Values

by Pamela J. Kuhn

D1306639

These pages may be copied.
Permission is granted to the buyer of this book to reproduce, duplicate or photocopy student materials in this book for use with pupils in Sunday school or Bible teaching classes.

Rainbow Publishers

Rainbow Publishers • P.O. Box 261129 • San Diego, CA 92196

Dedicated to...

My husband, RB, and my daughters Melanie and Emily. I hope your crowns are big enough to handle all of the jewels that are recommended by me.

INSTANT BIBLE LESSONS: VIRTUES AND VALUES

ISBN 1-885358-29-6
Rainbow reorder #36623

Rainbow Publishers
P.O. Box 261129
San Diego, CA 92196

Publisher: Arthur L. Miley
Illustrators: Joel Ryan, Roger Johnson
Editor: Christy Allen
Cover Design: Stray Cat Studio, San Diego, CA

Printed in the United States of America

Contents

Introduction

Virtues and Values teaches that all who are looking and longing for Christ to return will receive a crown of righteousness. Your class will be encouraged to live so their lives will be precious jewels to present to Christ when He appears. *Virtues and Values* contains dozens of activities based on those jewels, as described in the Bible. Each of the first eight chapters includes a Bible story, memory verse and numerous activities to help reinforce the truth in the lesson. An additional chapter contains miscellaneous projects that can be used anytime throughout the study. Teacher aids are also sprinkled throughout the book, including bulletin board ideas and discussion starters.

As you work through the lessons, you may use your own judgment as to the appropriateness of the projects for your class. Everything in this book is designed to meet the 5 to 10 age range, however some activities may be more appealing to a younger group while others will more readily meet the abilities of older children.

The most exciting aspect of the *Instant Bible Lessons* series, which includes *God's Angels, Bible Truths* and *Talking to God* as well as *Virtues and Values,* is its flexibility. You can easily adapt these lessons to a Sunday School hour, a children's church service, a Wednesday night Bible study or home use. And, because there is a variety of reproducible ideas from which to choose (see below), you will enjoy creating a class session that is best for your group of students—whether large or small, beginning or advanced, active or studious. Plus, the intriguing topics will keep your kids coming back for more, week after week.

This book is written to add fun and uniqueness to learning while reinforcing the anticipation of our crown of righteousness. Teaching children is exciting and rewarding. Okay, sometimes it's frustrating and challenging, but what joy results in obedience to the Bible: "Train up a child in the way he should go" (Proverbs 22:6). As a teacher, your crown will glisten with the jewel of faithfulness.

How to Use This Book

Each chapter begins with a Bible story which you may read to your class, followed by discussion questions. Then, use any or all of the activities in the chapter to help drive home the message of that lesson. All of the activities are tagged with one of the icons below, so you can quickly flip through the chapter and select the projects you need. Simply cut off the teacher instructions on the pages and duplicate as desired. Also, see pages 87 and 88 for reproducible notes you can fill in and send home to parents.

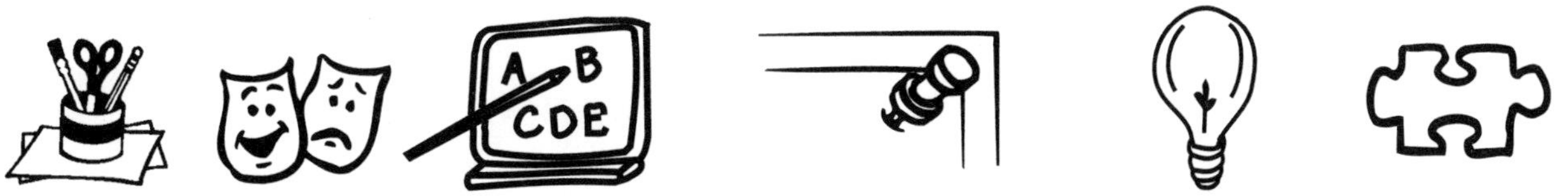

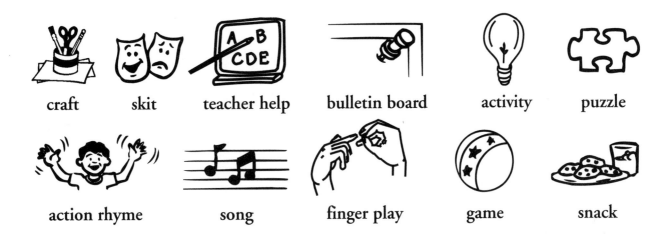

craft | skit | teacher help | bulletin board | activity | puzzle

action rhyme | song | finger play | game | snack

Chapter 1

God Gives Me a Crown

Memory Verse

There is in store for me the crown of righteousness, which the Lord…will award to me…and…to all who have longed for his appearing. 2 Timothy 4:8

Story to Share

Looking and Watching

James thought back over the past 40 days. So much had happened! Sadness crossed his face as he recalled the day Jesus was nailed to the cross. Jesus, who had never sinned, had suffered a painful death. He died to take the punishment for our sins.

Then a look of pure joy broke through the sadness as he remembered what happened three days after Jesus' death. James' brother, John, noticed the smile on James' face.

"James, what are you so happy about?" John asked his brother. "Did you get invited to Aunt Martha's for supper?"

Now that would've been something to smile about! Aunt Martha was known for her food. She could fry fish better than anyone. "No, John," James answered. "I was remembering the day Mary found the empty tomb."

Both brothers were lost in thought, remembering the joyous resurrection and the miracles and teachings of Jesus since that day. They walked along, their sandals filling with dust as they followed the resurrected Jesus to Bethany.

James and the other disciples gathered around Jesus. James felt the peace which was always with him when Jesus was near, but today that peace was mixed with anticipation.

"I want you, My disciples, to spread the news of My death and resurrection," Jesus instructed. "The Holy Spirit will come to give you power to spread the news throughout the land."

James watched in awe as Jesus was then lifted into the clouds. Stunned, none of the disciples moved.

"Why are you staring into heaven?" James heard. Turning, he saw two men dressed in white. "Jesus went to be with His Father, God," the men said. "One day He will return to you just as He went away."

Once again James was filled with joy — he was going to spread the Good News and watch for Jesus' return.

For those waiting for Jesus to return there is a promise of a crown — a crown of righteousness. Let's live like Jesus wants us to so our lives will be precious jewels to present to Him: jewels of compassion, cooperation, submission, determination, appreciation, conviction and adoration.

—based on Acts 1:3-11

Questions for Discussion

1. Are you watching for Jesus to come again?
2. What were the disciples supposed to do while they were waiting for Jesus? Can we do that today?

We're Looking for Jesus

bulletin board

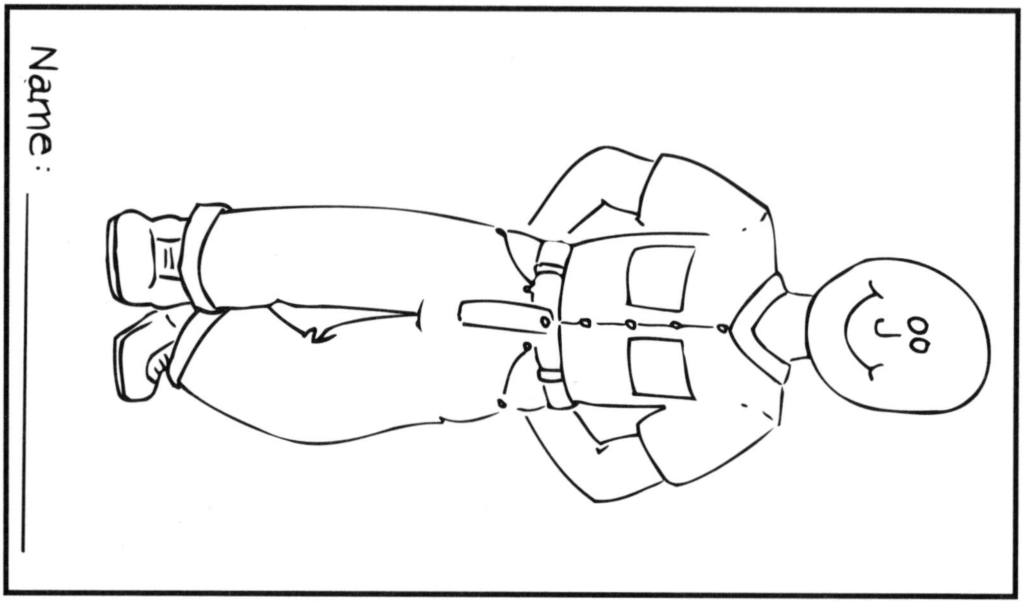

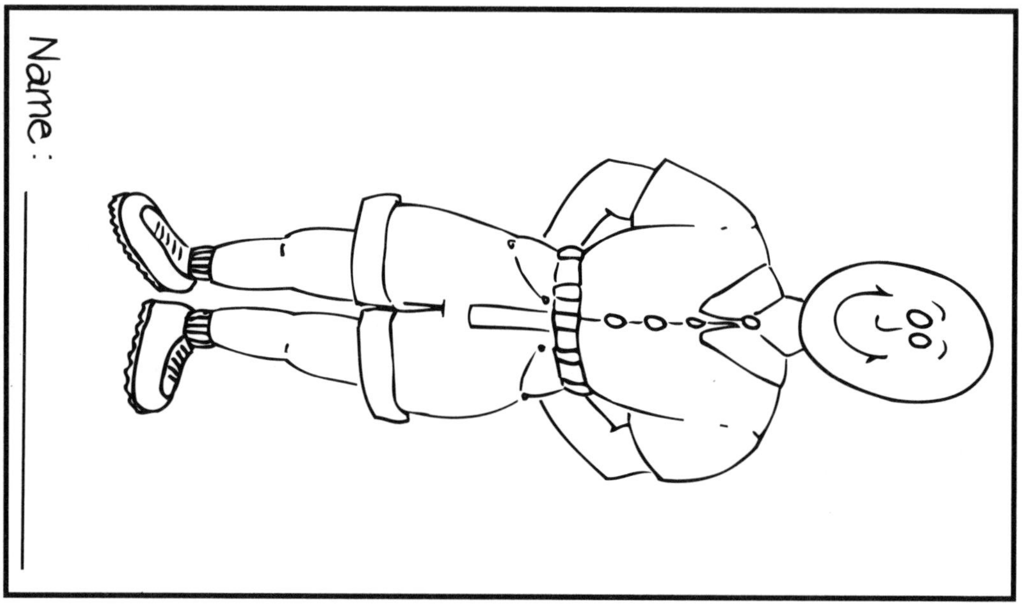

Materials

- •boys and girls patterns
- •crayons
- •scissors
- •glue
- •"We're Looking For Jesus" lettering

Directions

1. Have the children color a boy or girl figure to look like themselves, then cut it out on the box lines.
2. Post "We're Looking For Jesus" lettering at the top of the bulletin board.
3. Space the children figures around the bulletin board and attach.
4. See page 9 for an additional activity to add to this bulletin board.

Into the Clouds

I am looking
for Jesus
Name:

craft

Materials

- •illustration, duplicated
- •crayons
- •glue
- •cotton balls

Directions

1. Have the children color the picture of Jesus.
2. Show how to stretch the cotton balls and glue them to the cloud.
3. Say, **Write your name on the line if you are looking for Jesus to come back.**
4. This craft may be used with the p. 8 activity for a bulletin board display.

Presenting Myself to God

You can find out what God wants if you cross out these letters:

T, S, O, H, P, R, B, I, L, C, K, A, D, U

What is left that God wants?
Write the remaining letters on the line:

T O P B L O C K S M C A R D O L L E T R U C K S H I R T

____

I want to live my life for God.

____

(sign)

Solution is on page 96.

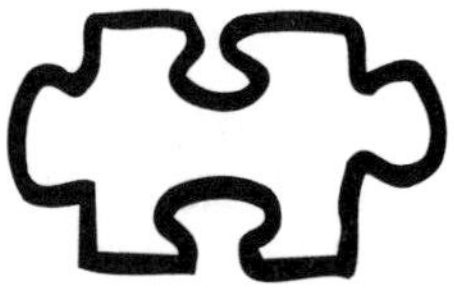

puzzle

Materials

- puzzle, duplicated
- pencils

Discuss

Say, **Do you have a favorite toy?** (Allow time for responses.) **What about favorite clothes? Does God want you to give your favorite things to Him? No, you don't have one thing that God wants. He only wants you.**

God Gives Me a Crown

Looking Glasses

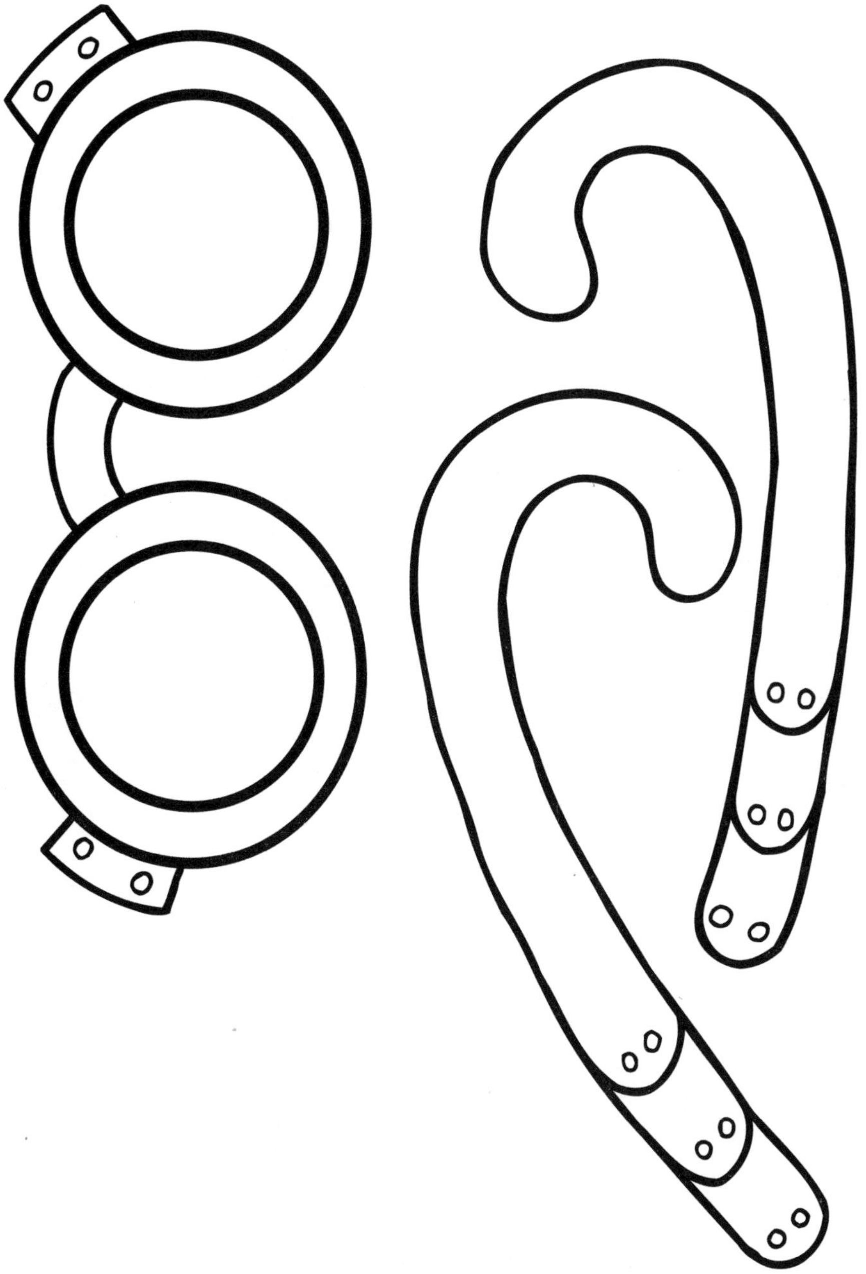

craft

Materials

- glasses, duplicated to heavy white paper
- scissors
- crayons
- colored cellophane paper, pre-cut
- tape or glue

Directions

1. Have the children color the glasses parts and cut them out.
2. Show how to carefully cut out the centers of the lenses.
3. Give each child two squares of cellophane and instruct the class to glue it behind each lens opening.
4. Help them to size the arms to fit their head by cutting off any excess. Then they may tape or glue the arms to the lens piece.
5. Have the children put on their glasses when you sing "Are You Looking?"

Pin the Crown on the Boy

game

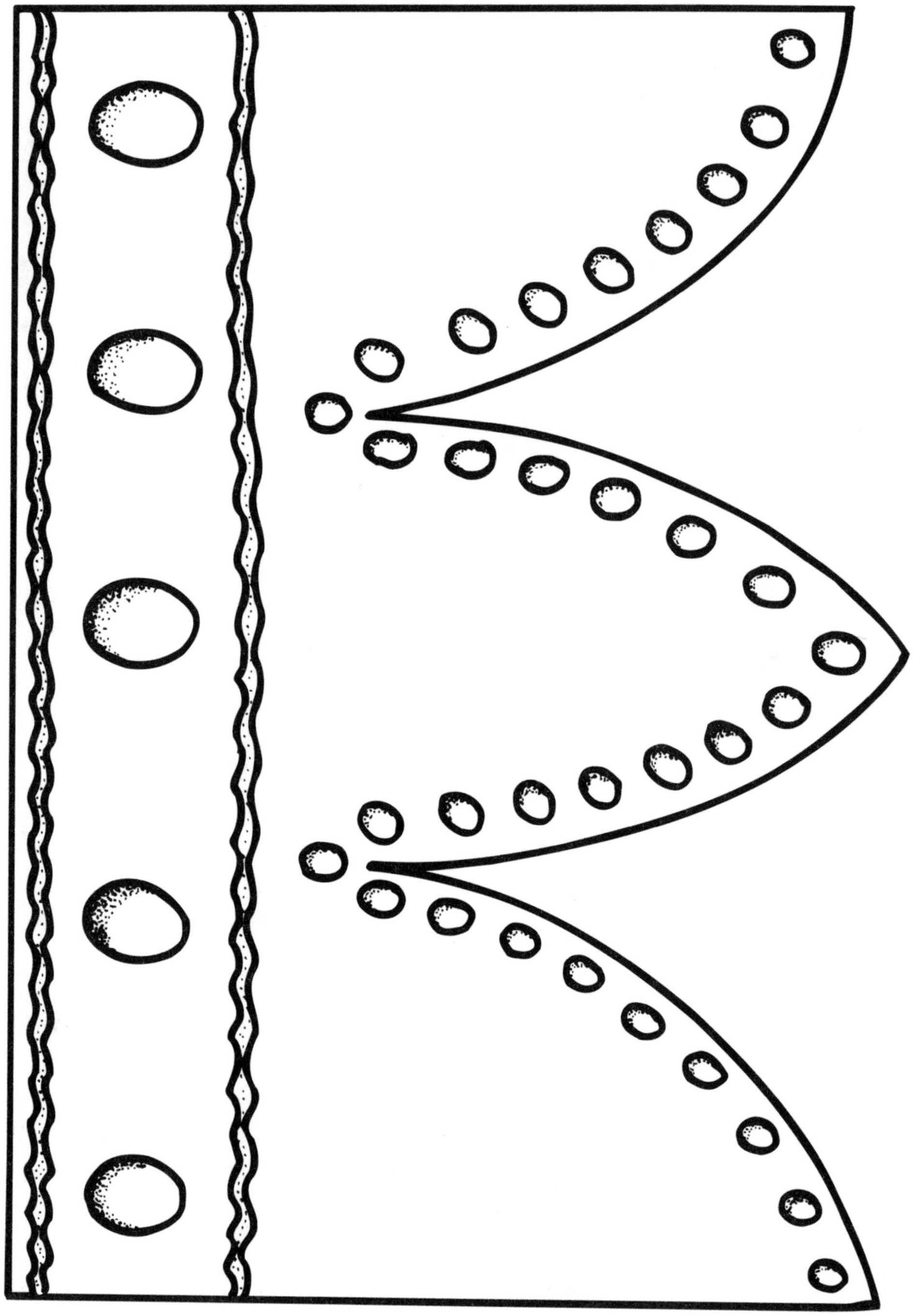

Materials

- •boy and crown, duplicated to gold paper
- •scissors
- •push pins or tape
- •blindfold

Directions

1. Color and cut out the boy and the crown.
2. Hang the boy on the bulletin board.
3. Choose a child to blindfold. Give him or her the crown.
4. As you turn the child around, say the memory verse together.
5. See how close to the boy's head the students can place the crown, similar to "Pin the Tail on the Donkey."

There is in store for me the crown of righteousness, which the Lord... will award to me...and...to all who have longed for his appearing.
2 Timothy 4:8

Chapter 2
My Jewel of Compassion

Memory Verse

His compassions never fail. They are new every morning; great is your faithfulness. Lamentations 3:22-23

Story to Share

Jesus' Great Compassion

Jesus and His disciples were on their way to Jerusalem. A great multitude of people followed them. As they passed through the edge of Jericho, they saw a blind man, Bartimaeus, begging beside the road.

Bartimaeus could not see, but he could hear. "Who is that crowd of people coming this way?" he asked.

"It's a lot of people following Jesus," a man answered quickly as he dropped a coin in Bartimaeus' hand.

"Jesus," breathed Bartimaeus. "Jesus, the man who heals people. I know He can make me see. I know He can."

Bartimaeus listened until he knew the crowd was close. "Jesus, Jesus, have mercy on me!" he cried loudly.

Those standing near him laughed and said, "Hush! Jesus doesn't want to hear from you."

But Bartimaeus couldn't be quiet when he knew Jesus could help him! He called again even louder, "Jesus, have mercy on me!"

Jesus heard Bartimaeus cry out to Him and stopped. With great compassion, he said, "Where is he who has called for help? Bring him to Me." Bartimaeus trembled as the crowd shouted for him to get up. He jumped up to be led to Jesus.

Bartimaeus knew it was Jesus by the kindness in His voice when He asked, "What do you want Me to do for you?" "Oh, my Lord, my Master, I would like to see," answered Bartimaeus breathlessly.

Jesus saw the faith in Bartimaeus' heart. He wanted to help this blind man. "Go on your way, Bartimaeus. You can see," He said. Bartimaeus looked up and saw the bright blue of the sky. Then he saw the smiles of the people around him. Joy and thanksgiving bubbled up out of Bartimaeus. He could not be still. With eyes that darted to and fro, never missing a sight, he followed Jesus. "Thank You for my sight. Thank You, Jesus, for my sight," he repeated.

The crowd that saw Jesus' compassion joined in his song of praise. "Praise God, praise God."

— based on Mark 10:46-52

Questions for Discussion

1. Can you make a blind man see?
2. What things can you do to show compassion?

Disciple, Disciple, Bartimaeus

game

Materials

- Bartimaeus, duplicated to heavy paper
- scissors
- self-stick, clear plastic

Directions

1. Color and cut out the figure and cover it with clear plastic.
2. Have the class sit in a circle and close their eyes. Select one child to be It. It walks around the circle, carrying Bartimaeus.
3. As It circles, he taps each child on the head and says Disciple.
4. At any time, It may say Bartimaeus instead of Disciple and drop the figure in that child's lap.
5. "Bartimaeus" grabs the figure, jumps up and says the memory verse before It runs around the circle and jumps in his space. If he cannot say the verse, he becomes It.

My Jewel of Compassion

Stand on Your Head!

The letters below are upside down!
Write the correct ones on the lines.
Then connect the dots to finish the picture.

HISƆOW dASSIONSNƎΛƎЯℲAI˥.THƎ⅄AЯƎNƎM

ƎΛƎЯ⅄WO ЯNIN⅁:GЯƎ⊥ATIS⅄O∩ЯℲAℲ⊥IHℲ∩˥NƎSS.

˥AWƎNTATIONSƐ:ZZ-ƐZ

____

____

____

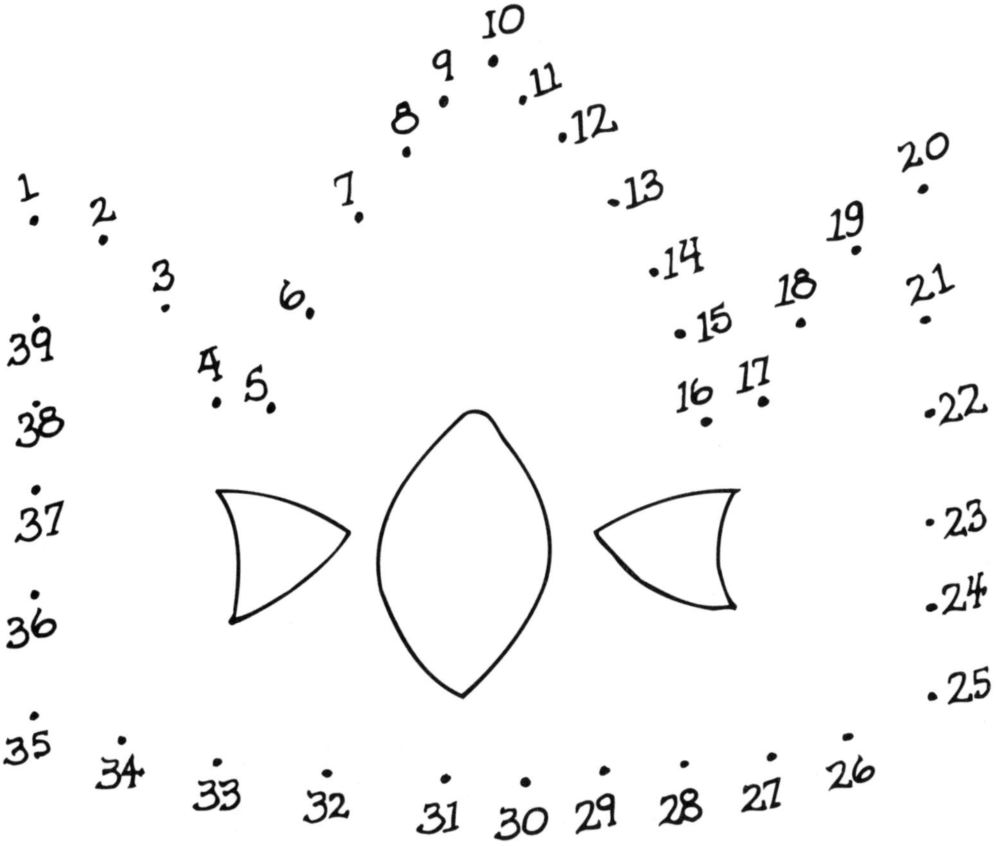

Solution is on page 96.

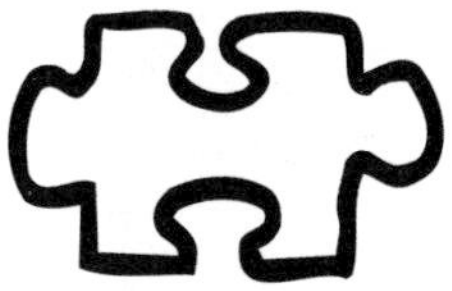

puzzle

Materials
- puzzle, duplicated
- pencils or markers

Usage

Have this sheet copied and ready for the children when they arrive as a "preview" of the day's lesson and the memory verse. Or, use this sheet to fill in extra time at the end of the lesson and reinforce the memory verse.

song

Directions

Sing to the tune of "Three Blind Mice." Teach the class the hand motions along with the song.

Poor Blind Man

Poor blind man. Poor blind man. *close eyes and hold out hand*
He begs for coins. He begs for coins.
He hears the crowd say, "Jesus is near."
Jesus can heal me, I have no fear.
Poor blind man. Poor blind man.

Help me, Lord. Help me, Lord. *hold finger to lips to say "shh"*
Make my blind eyes see. Make my blind eyes see.
"Don't yell, be quiet," the crowd does say.
There's no time here for you today.
Help me, Lord. Help me, Lord.

Jesus cares. Jesus cares. *hand up, calling out*
He has compassion. He has compassion.
He hears the blind man call to Him.
"Bring him here," He says to them.
Jesus cares. Jesus cares.

Bartimaeus. Bartimaeus. *point to open eyes*
He can see. He can see.
The man was given his sight that day.
Now he can see the children play.
Bartimaeus. Bartimaeus.

Praise His name! Praise His name! *raise hands in praise*
I can see. I can see.
I can see the flowers and the trees.
The butterflies, the buzzing bees.
Praise His name! Praise His name!

Blind Man's Cup Review

His compassions never fail. - Lamentations 3:22

Review Questions

1. Where were Jesus and His disciples going? (Jerusalem)
2. Who was following them? (a multitude of people)
3. What city were they passing through? (Jericho)
4. Who was sitting beside the road? (Bartimaeus)
5. What was wrong with Bartimaeus? (He was blind.)
6. What was he doing there? (begging)
7. When Bartimaeus found out Jesus was coming, what did he say? (He will make me see.)
8. Were the people around Bartimaeus happy about his calling to Jesus? (no)
9. What did Jesus say when He heard Bartimeaus call out? (Bring him to Me.)
10. How did Jesus show compassion to Bartimeaus? (He healed him.)
11. What did Bartimaeus do when he could see? (He thanked Jesus.)
12. What did the crowd do when they saw Jesus' great compassion? (They praised God.)

game

Materials

- verse strip, duplicated
- foam cups
- crayons
- scissors
- glue
- stickers
- pennies or candy coins

Directions

1. Have the class cut out and color the strip, then glue it around the rim of a foam cup (cut the questions from the page before duplicating for the class).
2. Allow the children to decorate their cups with crayons and stickers.
3. Ask the students the questions at left. Drop a coin in the cups of those who answer the questions correctly. Ask the questions more than once to reinforce the lesson and to give each child a chance to answer several.

Blind Man's Face

game

Materials

- head figure, duplicated twice
- crayons
- tape
- blindfolds

Directions

1. If possible, enlarge the head.
2. Tape the heads to the wall. Place extra paper around them to avoid marking the wall.
3. Divide the children into teams of two. Blindfold them and give them crayons.
4. Say, "Go." The first child walks to a head and draws eyes then returns.
5. Continue in a similar manner, drawing a nose, mouth, ears and hair.
6. The first team finished says the memory verse and removes the blindfolds.

Discuss

Ask, **How would it feel to be blind? What would you miss seeing? How can we help those in need?**

My Jewel of Compassion

Helping Others

My name is Bartimaeus.
I was blind, I was sad.
Then Jesus had compassion.
Now I can see, I am glad.

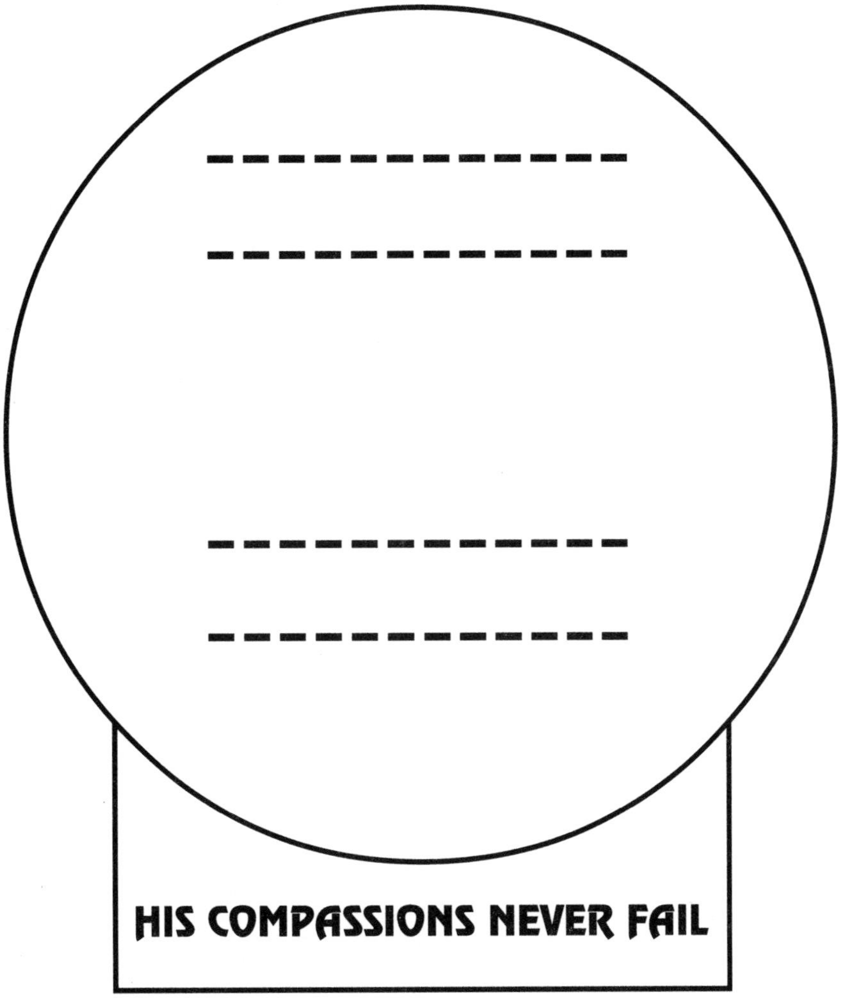
HIS COMPASSIONS NEVER FAIL

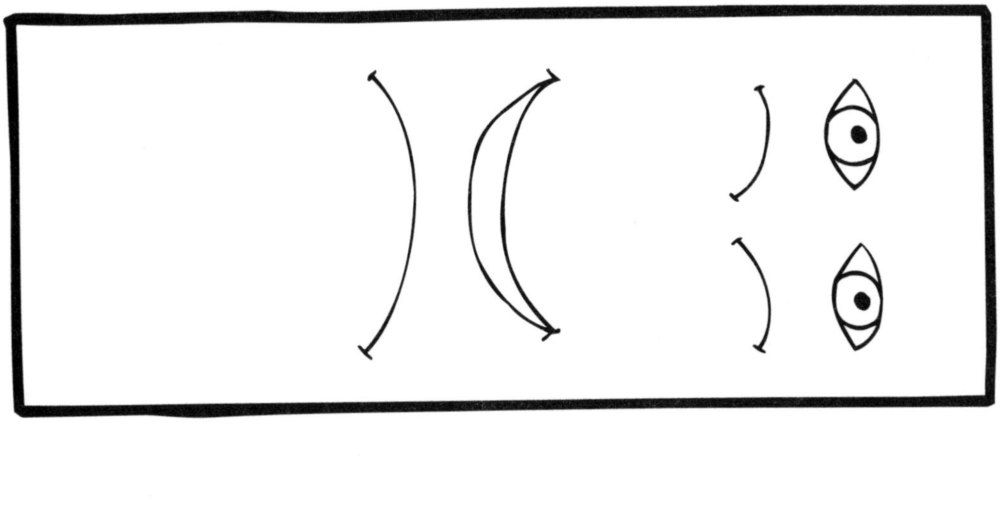

craft

Materials

- face and features strip, duplicated
- crayons
- scissors

Directions

1. Have the students color the Bartimaeus face and strip and cut them out.
2. Show how to cut the dashed lines on Bartimaeus' face.
3. Demonstrate how to weave the feature strip through the face, changing from sad and blind to happy and sighted.
4. Say the poem at the top of the page as the students change the faces.

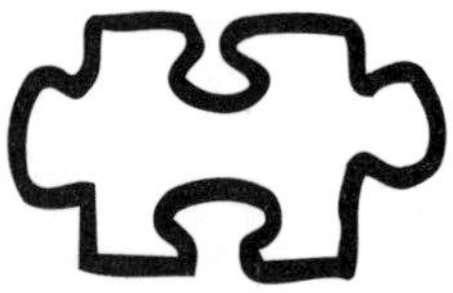

puzzle

Materials

- •puzzle, duplicated
- •pencils

Usage

This puzzle is a good opener to a discussion of "compassion," a big word for young children. Give many examples of the word's meaning so your students are sure to understand its usage. After you have explained the word, ask them to use it in a sentence to test their comprehension of this important concept.

My Jewel of Compassion

Compassion

What is it when you share the hurts of others?
What is it when you help those who are hurting?
Find out by writing the letter in the alphabet that comes before the letter below each line, then circle the mystery word.
HINT: It's the second word.

__ __ __   __ __ __ __ __ __ __ __ __ __
I J T   D P N Q B T T J P O T

__ __ __ __ __   __ __ __ __.   __ __ __ __
O F W F S   G B J M   U I F Z

__ __ __   __ __ __   __ __ __ __ __
B S F   O F X   F W F S Z

__ __ __ __ __ __ __;   __ __ __ __ __
N P S O J O H   H S F B U

__ __   __ __ __ __
J T   Z P V S

__ __ __ __ __ __ __ __ __ __ __ __.
G B J U I G V M O F T T

— Lamentations 3:22-23

Solution is on page 96.

Here I Come!

Follow the path to Jesus by writing down every other word on the lines below, starting left and going right.

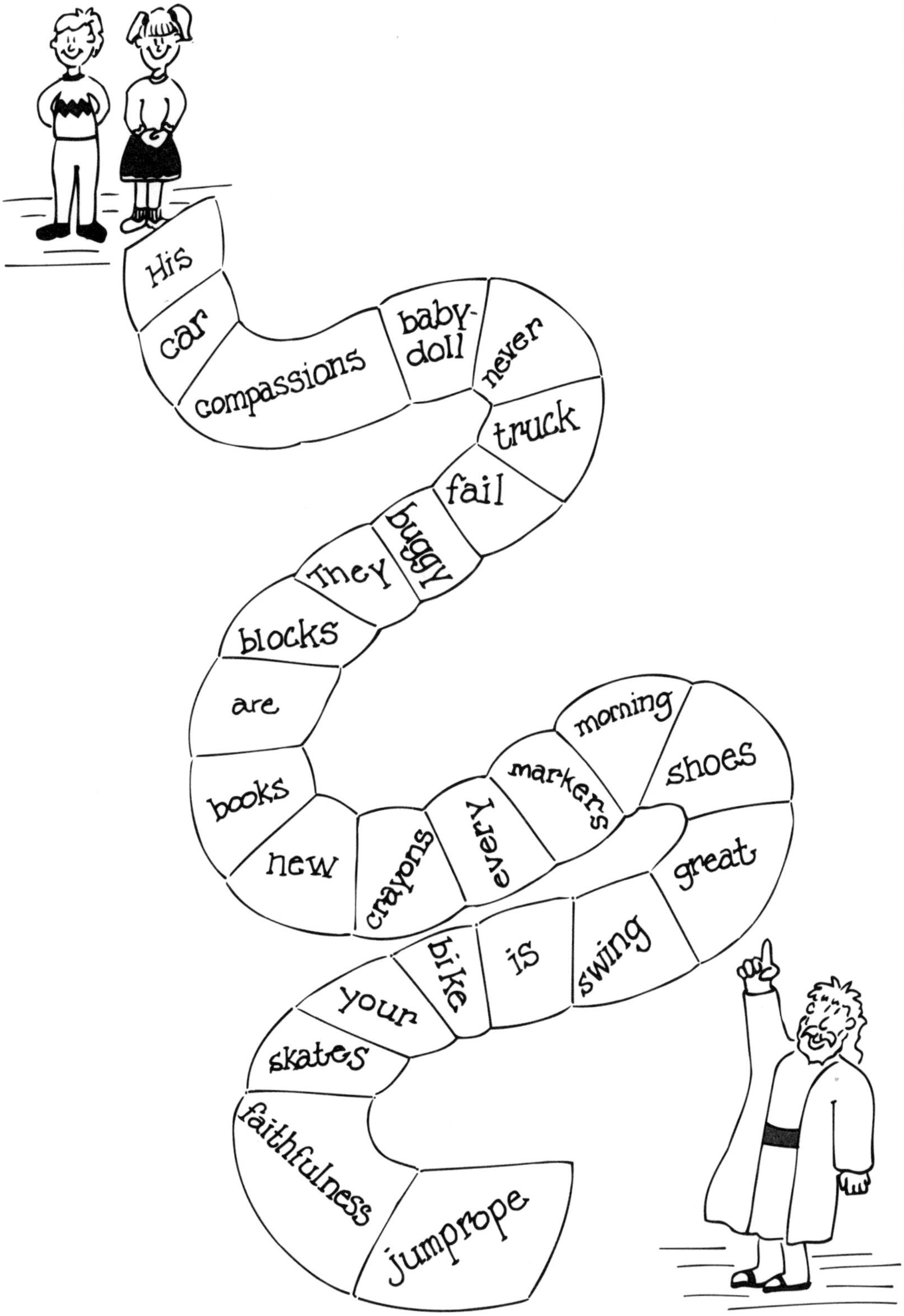

Solution is on page 96.

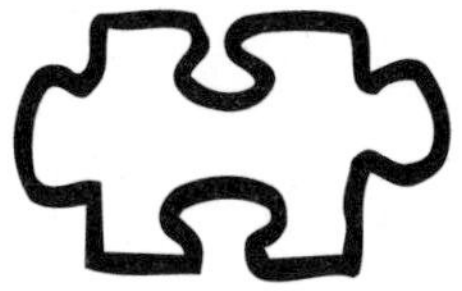

puzzle

Materials

- puzzle, duplicated
- pencils

Usage

This chapter includes three puzzles (see also pp. 19 and 24) that focus on the memory verse because it can be complicated for young children. Consider using this puzzle to review each word or phrase individually to assure understanding.

Chapter 3
My Jewel of Cooperation

Memory Verse

The whole body...grows and builds itself up in love, as each part does its work. Ephesians 4:16

Story to Share
Working Together

"It is necessary for us to cooperate!" insisted Nehemiah. "If we do, Jerusalem can be rebuilt quickly and efficiently."

Cyrus, king of Persia, had issued a proclamation that any captive Judeans who wished to return to Judah should be given their freedom. The king also returned the silver and gold treasure that was stolen from the temple by the Babylonians.

God's people were glad to return. But they were sad when they inspected the fallen walls and the gates that were destroyed by fire.

"Cooperate with me," Nehemiah again begged the men who were with him. "Let's rebuild Jerusalem! Our once-great city is a disgrace. Let's ask God to help us in our work."

"Yes, we will. We will help," said the people. Everyone joined together in the work. But soon, other people began to laugh at them.

"Look at those Israelites. What do they think they are doing?" said one. "Haven't you heard?" replied another, laughing. "They're rebuilding the temple. Have you ever heard anything so ridiculous in your life? Walls out of rubble!"

But the Israelites endured. It wasn't until the terrorism began that they became discouraged.

"Don't be afraid," urged Nehemiah. "The Lord is with us and will protect us."

He gave spears and shields to half of the workers. "Protect all of the workers," he instructed them.

Working together, some rebuilding the walls, others guarding those working, the repairs continued. The walls were finished in 52 days. Even the Israelites' enemies were forced to acknowledge that God had been with the Israelites.

— based on Nehemiah 4:6-16; 6:15-16

Questions for Discussion

1. Is it hard for you to cooperate?
2. How do you respond when your parents ask you to help? Your teacher?

Cooperation Books

craft

Materials

- illustration, duplicated
- white paper
- construction paper
- crayons or markers
- scissors
- stapler

Directions

1. Have the class color and cut out the illustration and glue it to the center of a horizontal piece of construction paper.
2. Distribute paper to each child and have them number the pages.
3. Assign a page number and a different scene from the story on p. 27 to each child. Have the children go around the room and draw their assigned scene in each book, until all books have scenes telling the story. If you have a large class, split them into work groups.
4. Have everyone return to their own books, add a piece of construction paper to the back and staple along the edge to make a book.

Cooperation
Helps Rebuild

Building Together

song

Directions
Sing to the tune of "The Wheels On The Bus Go Round and Round."

Discuss
Ask, What are the ways we build the church? Does the pianist work together with the organist? Does the janitor have his part to do? Who else works together? What is your part?

Jerusalem's walls came tumbling down,

clap hands

Tumbling down, tumbling down.

Jerusalem's walls came tumbling down.

Nehemiah was sad.

The people worked to build the walls,

build with fists

Build the walls, build the walls.

The people worked to build the walls.

Nehemiah was glad.

Let's work together to build the church,

continue building

Build the church, build the church.

Let's work together to build the church.

Working with love.

hug your neighbor

My Jewel of Cooperation

It Takes Us All

The children below couldn't have made
their pyramid if everyone wouldn't have cooperated.
Write the words of the memory verse on each one's shirt.
Write the book of the Bible and the scripture reference on the flags.
Memorize it!

activity

Materials

- activity, duplicated
- pencils
- crayons

Usage

Be sure the students have a good grasp of the memory verse before starting this activity. You may want to write the verse on the chalkboard, or write some of the words on the board as "hints." Provide crayons for the students to color the illustration after they fill in the memory verse words.

King Cooperation

craft

Materials

- strips, duplicated
- glue
- paper grocery sacks
- scissors
- markers
- faux jewels or beads
- stapler
- tape

Directions

1. Have the class cut off the bottoms of the bags, leaving a 10" tube.
2. Show how to fold 1" to the inside of the tube.
3. Help the students cut V-shapes a-round the top to form the crown.
4. They may color, cut out and glue on the King Coop-eration strips.
5. Assist the students as they put on their crowns. A tuck may be sta-pled in the back to fit smaller heads. Be sure to cover staples with tape to avoid scratching.

snack

Materials

- large marshmallows
- peanut butter
- small paper cups
- plastic knives
- waxed paper
- paper plates
- scissors
- glue
- crayons

Directions

1. Give each child some waxed paper, marshmallows, a some peanut butter in a cup and a plastic knife.
2. Show how to spread peanut butter on the bottom of a marshmallow and stick it to the top of another one on a paper plate, then spread peanut butter on its side to attach more.
3. Allow the children to continue to build a "wall."
4. The students may color, cut out and glue the figures at right to the plate to create a scene. They may eat their wall, or you may bring extra marshmallows for snacking.

My Jewel of Cooperation

Marshmallow Walls

Add and Solve

To whom can we turn when we need encouragement to cooperate?
Use your math to find out!
Add up each equation, then place that equation's letter
on the line above the number that matches the equation's total.

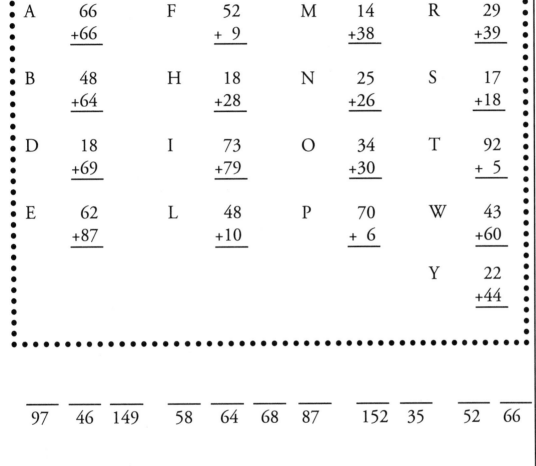

A	66 +66	F	52 + 9	M	14 +38	R	29 +39
B	48 +64	H	18 +28	N	25 +26	S	17 +18
D	18 +69	I	73 +79	O	34 +30	T	92 + 5
E	62 +87	L	48 +10	P	70 + 6	W	43 +60
						Y	22 +44

___ ___ ___   ___ ___ ___ ___   ___ ___   ___ ___
97 46 149   58 64 68 87   152 35   52 66

___ ___ ___ ___ ___ ___;   ___   ___ ___ ___ ___
46 149 58 76 149 68   152   103 152 58 58

___ ___ ___   ___ ___   ___ ___ ___ ___ ___ ___.
51 64 97   112 149   132 61 68 132 152 87

___ ___ ___ ___ ___ ___ ___   13:6
46 149 112 68 149 103 35

Solution is on page 96.

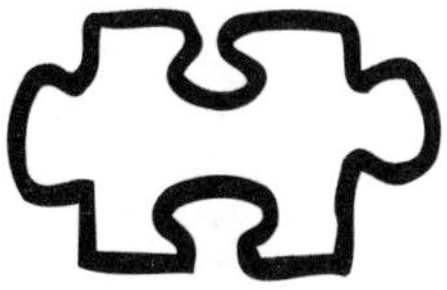

puzzle

Materials

- puzzle, duplicated
- pencils

Usage

Kids love solving codes, so promote this puzzle as a sleuth-type activity. Be available to help those whose math skills may not be as strong as others'. Allow your older students who finish first to assist younger or slower children if necessary, emphasizing their actions as examples of the jewel of cooperation.

My Jewel of Cooperation

Blocks of Cooperation

activity

Materials

- block strips, duplicated to heavy white paper
- scissors
- crayons
- tape

Directions

1. Have the children write the names of people with whom they can cooperate on the blocks.
2. Allow them to color and cut them out. You may distribute as many sheets of blocks as desired.
3. Show how to form the blocks by folding inward at the dashed line and taping together.
4. Say, **What can you build with your blocks of cooperation?**

Discuss

Say, **The rebuilding of Jerusalem could not have happened without cooperation. Can you think of some ways you can cooperate at home? At school? At play?**

My Jewel of Cooperation

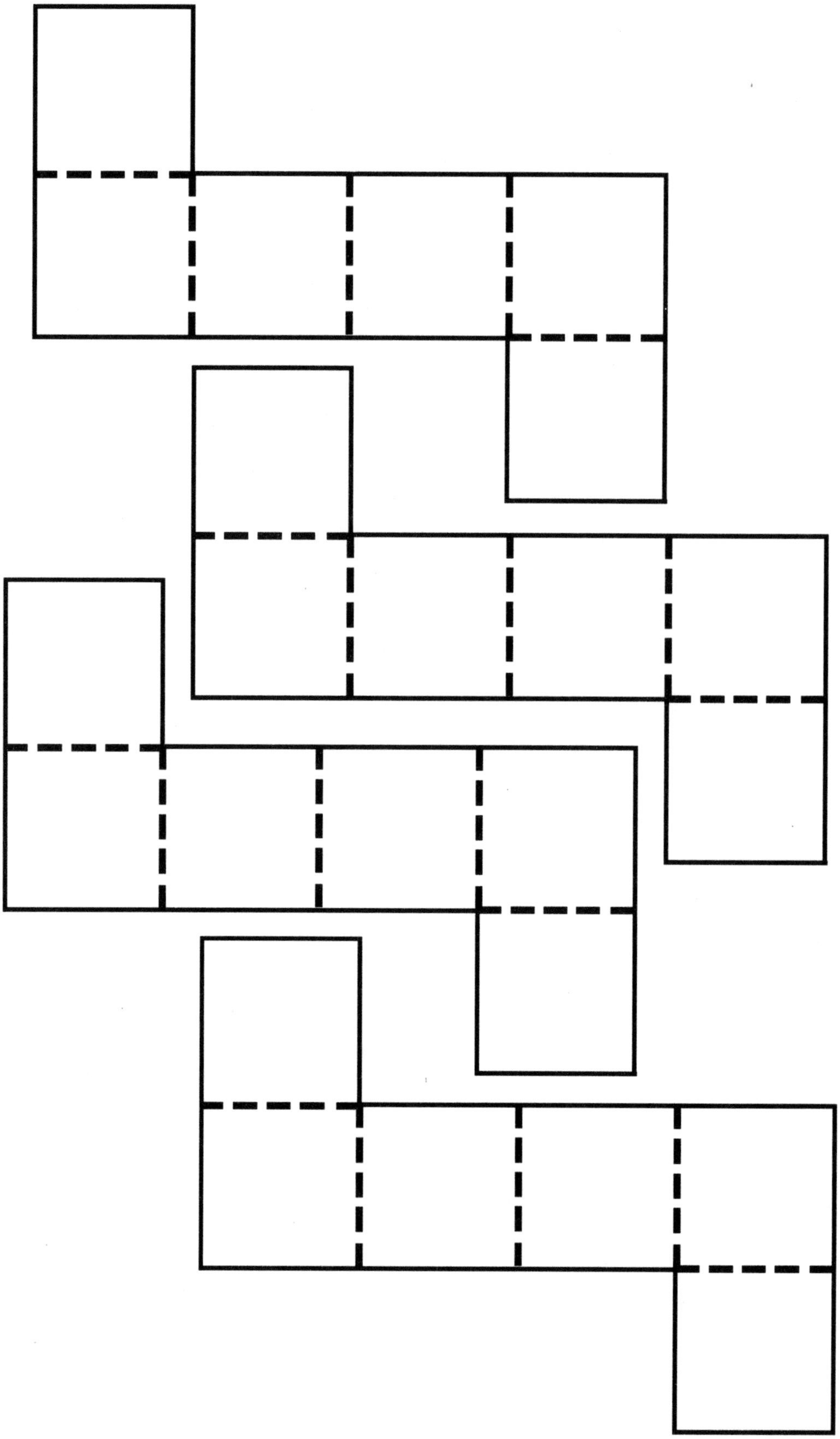

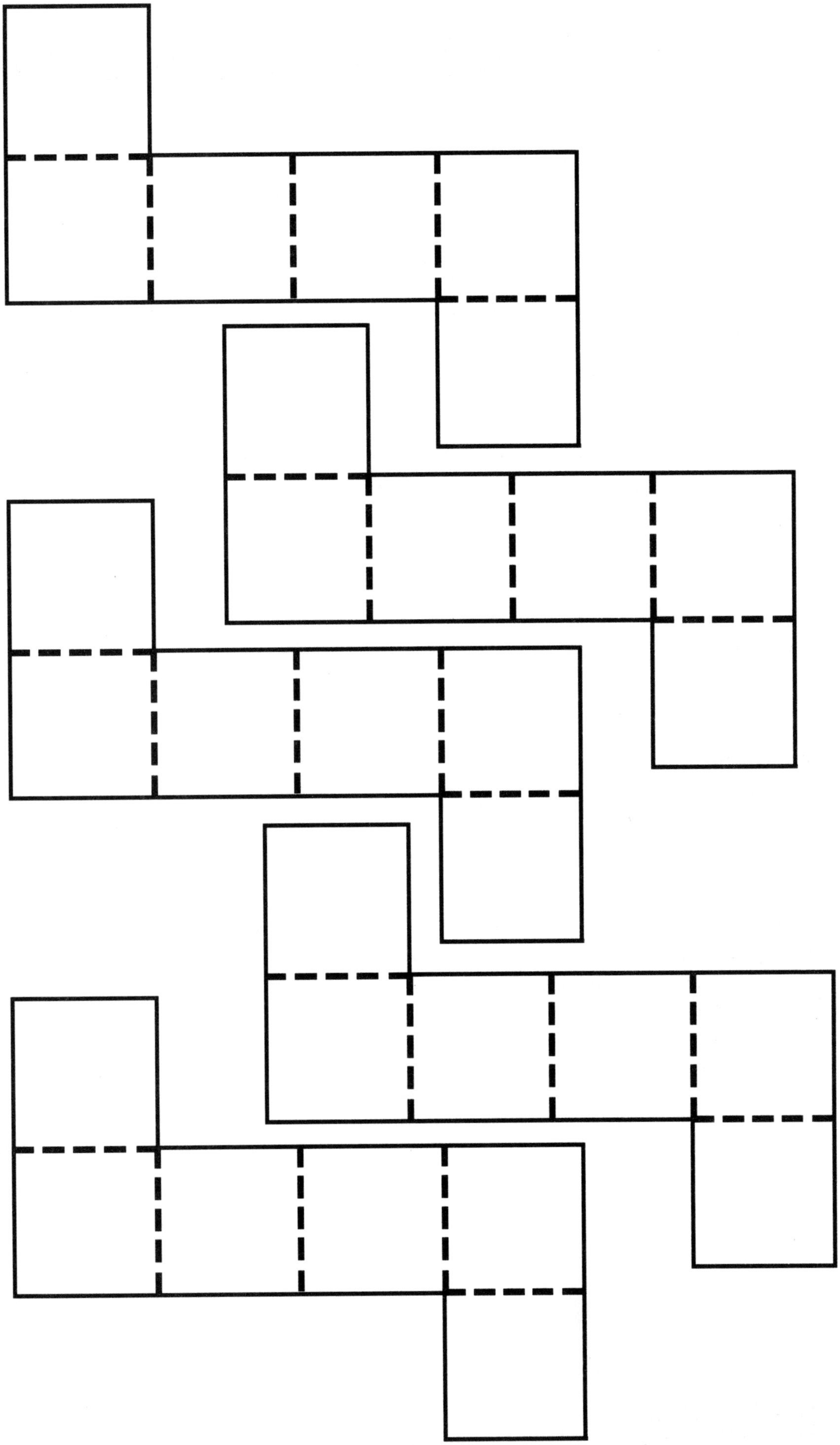

Chapter 4
My Jewel of Submission

Memory Verse

Young men…be submissive to those who are older. 1 Peter 5:5

Story to Share

Submission? No Way!

"I will be the next king of Israel," Absalom secretly schemed. "Nobody, not even my father, David, will stand in my way." But Absalom knew that Solomon was David's chosen heir, not him.

Absalom was an exceptionally handsome man with long, thick hair. But he was extremely rebellious and hot-headed. He even quarreled with his half-brother and killed him. Absalom was sent into hiding, but after a while his father, King David, allowed him to return to Jerusalem.

Absalom bought a chariot and horses. Every morning he stood at the city gate, talking to those who came to see the king. He was likable and popular.

"Now is my time," Absalom said after four years. "Now I will be king of Israel."

In Hebron, Absalom raised a powerful army and challenged his father to a battle for the throne. It was a long battle. Hundreds of men were killed. The rebels were chased out of the city.

Absalom jumped on the back of a mule. The mule, frightened by the noise of fighting, bolted into the shelter of the forest. Galloping wildly through the trees, Absalom's long hair was caught in the branches of an oak tree. Off the mule galloped, leaving Absalom dangling in the tree by his hair, unable to free himself.

"Joab, Joab," a soldier in David's army said to the commander. "Absalom is swinging from a tree. I did not touch him because he is King David's son."

"King David's son? His rebellion will only be finished when he is dead," replied Joab. Grabbing three spears, Joab rode to where Absalom was hanging. With mighty thrusts, Joab drove the spears into Absalom's chest.

"Throw his body into that pit and cover it with stones," directed Joab, who acted against the direction of Absalom's father, King David. The king had commanded that Absalom be spared in the battle. But Joab viewed Absalom as a threat to the king so he killed him anyway.

What a great price Absalom paid for rebellion against his father! Absalom's lack of submission cost him his life. King David mourned the death of his son, even though he had severely disobeyed him.

— based on 2 Samuel 15; 18:6-16

Questions for Discussion

1. Can you think of a time when you didn't do what your parents or teachers said and you got into trouble?
2. Do your parents and teachers know what is best for you?

I Will Be Submissive!

craft

Materials

- •bee pattern, duplicated
- •crayons
- •scissors
- •hole punch
- •yarn

Directions

1. Have the class cut out and color the bee and punch a hole at the top dot.
2. Instruct them to write the names of people they will submit to on the bee's wings.
3. Cut a length of yarn for each student. Show how to thread yarn through the hole and tie the ends together.
4. Say, **Wear your bee so all your friends will know you will Bee Submissive.**

Name
Young men... be submissive to those who are older. 1 Peter 5:5
I WILL BEE SUBMISSIVE

Submission Contract Card

Young men…be submissive to those who are older. 1 Peter 5:5

craft

Materials

- •illustration, duplicated
- •construction paper, light colors
- •glue
- •crayons or markers
- •scissors

Directions

1. Show the students how to fold a piece of construction paper in half like a card.
2. Allow them to color and cut out the illustration, then glue it to the inside of the folded paper.
3. On the outside of the card, help them write I WILL…
4. On the inside, help them sign their name on the line.
5. Tell the class to present their Contract Cards to their parents as a commitment to submission.

Submissive Bee Snacks

snack

Materials

- •recipe, duplicated
- •½ cup of peanut butter
- •1 tablespoon of honey
- •⅓ cup of nonfat powdered milk
- •1 teaspoon of cocoa powder
- •2 tablespoons of sesame seeds
- •sliced almonds
- •waxed paper

Directions

1. Give each child some waxed paper. Depending on the size of your group, you may need to increase the recipe.
2. Mix the peanut butter and honey.
3. Stir in the powdered milk, cocoa and sesame seeds until well mixed.
4. Give each child a teaspoon of dough and two almond slices.
5. Show how to shape the dough into ovals to look like bees. Stick almonds in the side for wings.
6. Distribute the recipes to take home.

SUBMISSIVE BEE SNACK

INGREDIENTS

- •½ cup of peanut butter
- •1 tablespoon of honey
- •⅓ cup of nonfat powdered milk
- •1 teaspoon of cocoa powder
- •2 tablespoons of sesame seeds
- •sliced almonds

YOU WILL ALSO NEED

- •bowl
- •spoon
- •measuring cups and spoons
- •waxed paper

INSTRUCTIONS

Mix the peanut butter and honey together in a bowl. Stir in the powdered milk, cocoa and sesame seeds until well mixed. Place one teaspoon of dough for each bee on waxed paper. Shape the dough into an oval, like a bee's body, and stick almonds in the sides for wings. No cooking required—just eat and enjoy!

Young men...be submissive to those who are older. 1 Peter 5:5

Jewels of Submission

The verse below is missing some very important jewels.
Can you cut them out and glue them where they belong?

"Young ____________ ...be ______________

to ____________ who are ____________."

1 ____________ 5:5

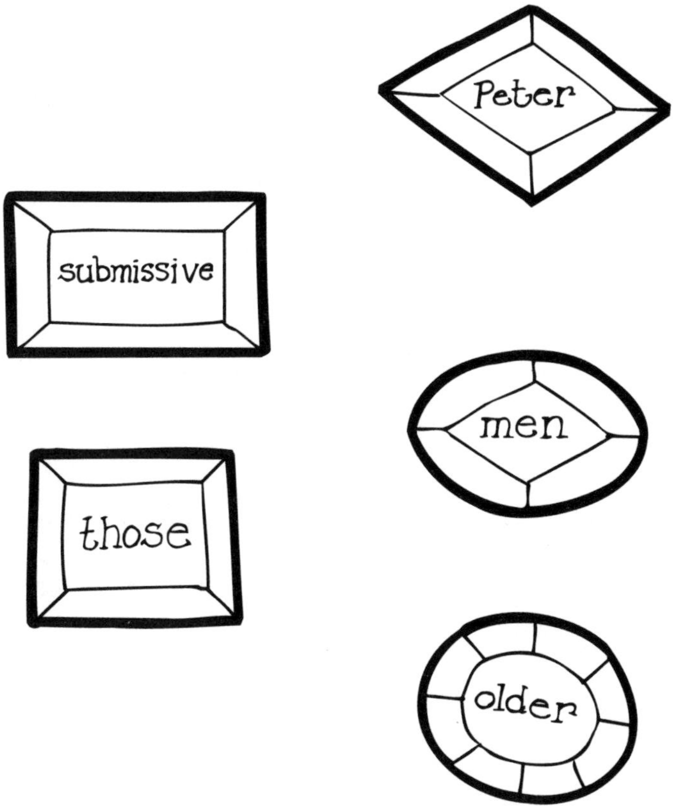

Solution is on page 96.

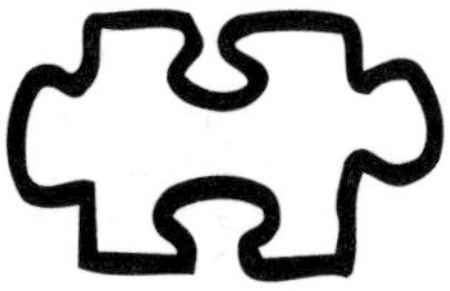

puzzle

Materials

- puzzle, duplicated
- scissors
- tape or glue

Discuss

Ask, **What is submission? It is obeying those in authority over us, instead of doing what we want to do. Who has authority over us? Who is the most important person we should obey?**

My Jewel of Submission

song

Directions

Sing to the tune of "The Wise Man and the Foolish Man." The song sheets in this book, like all other pages, may be photocopied for the children to color and take home as lesson reminders. Or, tear them out and keep them together as a terrific collection of easy, meaningful songs to use year-round in your class!

Rebellion Should Be Banned

There was a man who wanted to be king.
There was a man who wanted to be king.
There was a man who wanted to be king.
Submission was not his thing.

The wise man fought with God on his side.
The wise man fought with God on his side.
The wise man fought with God on his side.
But soldiers were hurt and died.

The foolish man's hair got caught up in a tree.
The foolish man's hair got caught up in a tree.
The foolish man's hair got caught up in a tree.
And he died before he got free.

Submission to elders is God's command.
Submission to elders is God's command.
Submission to elders is God's command.
Rebellion should be banned!

Tied Up

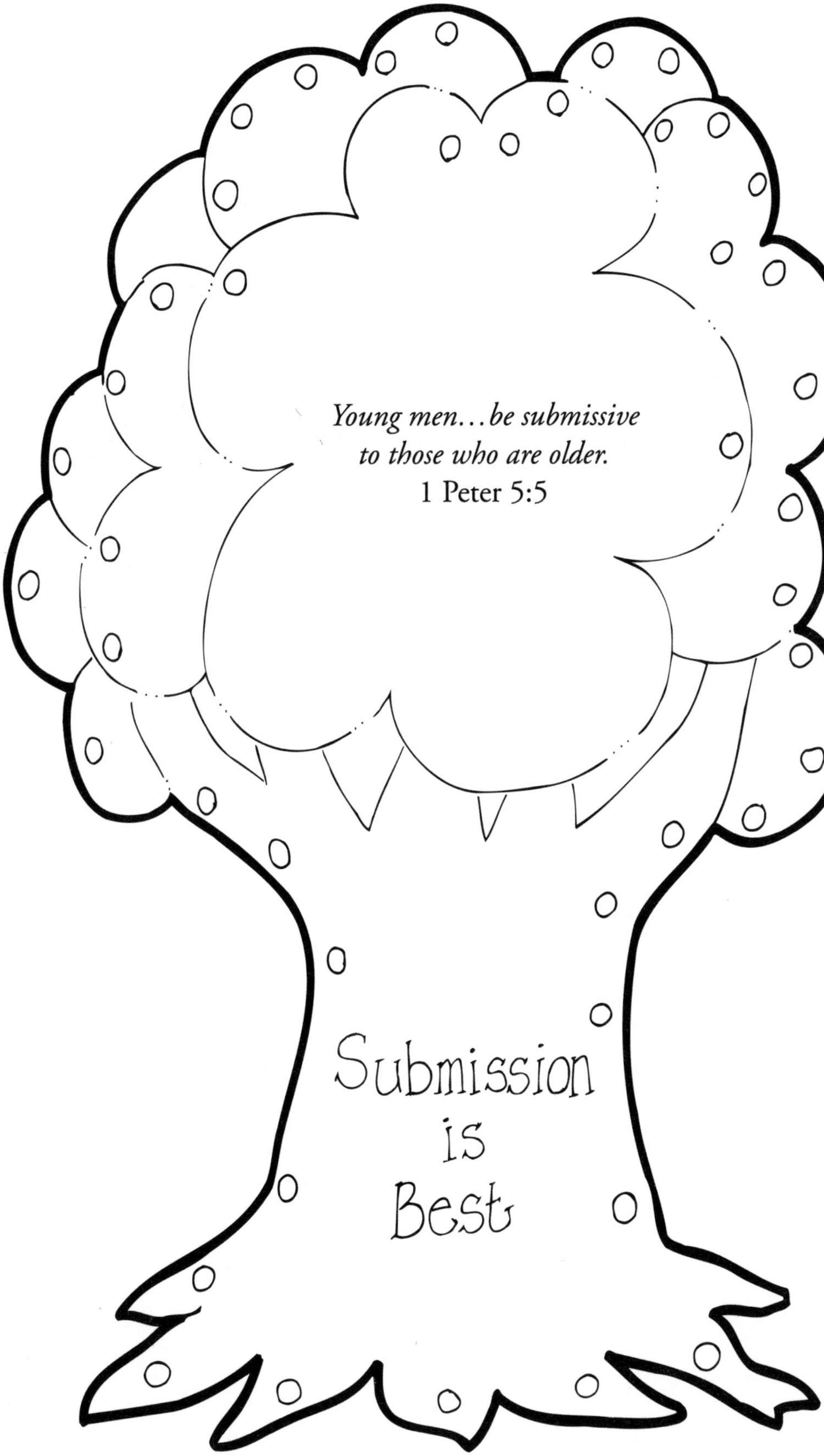

Young men... be submissive to those who are older.
1 Peter 5:5
Submission is Best

craft

Materials

- tree, duplicated to heavy paper
- crayons
- hole punch
- yarn
- tape
- scissors
- clear, self-stick paper

Directions

1. Have the class color and cut out the tree.
2. Show how to cover it with sticky paper.
3. Have the students punch the holes where indicated.
4. Cut a length of yarn for each child. To make stitching easier, allow them to wrap a piece of tape around the ends of the yarn.
5. Help the children thread the yarn in one hole and tie with a knot at the back.
6. Show how to sew in and out of the holes to "stitch" the tree.

My Jewel of Submission

Tic-Tac-Toe Crowns

craft/game

Materials

- tree and crowns, duplicated
- crayons
- scissors

Directions

1. Have the students color and cut out the tree and crowns.
2. Write the following words on the chalkboard: mule, Absalom, Solomon, king of Israel, Joab, yes, no, halfbrother, hair, submission, David, three spears, tree.
3. Instruct the class to choose nine of the words and write them on their game board tree. No two boards should be exactly alike.
4. Ask the questions at right. Those who have the correct answer on their boards should place a crown over that word.
5. When someone gets three in a row, he or she should stand up and shout "Submission!"

My Jewel of Submission

Questions

1. Who in our lesson was rebellious? (Absalom)
2. What did he want to be? (king of Israel)
3. Who was the present king? (David)
4. Who did David intend to be the next king? (Solomon)
5. Who did Absalom kill? (Amnon, his half-brother)
6. Absalom challenged his father, David, to a battle. Did Absalom win? (no)
7. What was Absalom riding when when he ran from the fighting? (a mule)
8. What was caught in the tree which made Absalom unable to free himself? (his hair)
9. Who killed Absalom? (Joab)
10. What did Joab use to kill Absalom? (3 spears)
11. Absalom's lack of what caused him to lose his life? (submission)

Chapter 5
My Jewel of Determination

Memory Verse
I am convinced... that [nothing] will be able to separate us from the love of God. Romans 8:38-39

Story to Share
Jesus – In Spite of Death

"Stephen," one of the apostles said, "we are so busy teaching about Jesus. There just isn't time to take care of our followers as we should. Would you be willing to oversee the feeding of the widows? These women whose husbands have died don't always get their share of food."

Stephen, who loved God, did not hesitate. "Yes, I will be happy to serve in any way I can," he said.

Stephen did his job with joy. He also preached, and God worked miracles through him. He brought many people to follow in Jesus' footsteps. This angered the Jewish elders and they brought him before the council.

"We have heard this man speak blasphemous words against Moses and God," lied the elders. "He says Jesus of Nazareth intends to destroy Jerusalem."

"What?" the high priest exclaimed. "Is this what you said?"

"You have chosen not to listen to God's desires," Stephen calmly told them. "You killed God's Son when He came to save you."

The council members were furious. Glaring at Stephen with their teeth clenched in anger, they saw him looking upward. "I see the glory of God in Heaven, and Jesus standing by His right side," Stephen said with a glow on his face.

This outraged the elders even more. They covered their ears so they did not have to hear what Stephen was saying. Yelling angrily, they rushed at Stephen, dragging him outside the city walls. Picking up stones, they hurled them at Stephen.

As the pain filled his body, Stephen cried out, "Lord Jesus, forgive these people." Then he died, the determination to serve Jesus, whether in life or death, firmly rooted in his heart.

— based on Acts 6; 7:54-60

Questions for Discussion

1. Are you determined to be a Christian?
2. Will you take a stand when everyone else wants to do something that is wrong?

Hurtful Stones

activity

Materials

- activity, duplicated
- glitter pens
- markers

Directions

1. Have the children outline the heart with glitter pens.
2. Instruct them to write ways that they have been hurt by others on the lines in front of the stones.
3. Say, **If you are determined to be a Christian, regardless of what anyone says or does to you, write your name in the heart.**

Discuss

Say, **Perhaps no one has ever thrown stones at you, but there are other ways we can be hurt. Has anyone ever called you names? Ever told things about you that weren't true? What are other things people can do to hurt us? Let's make sure we're not doing those things to anyone!**

My Jewel of Determination

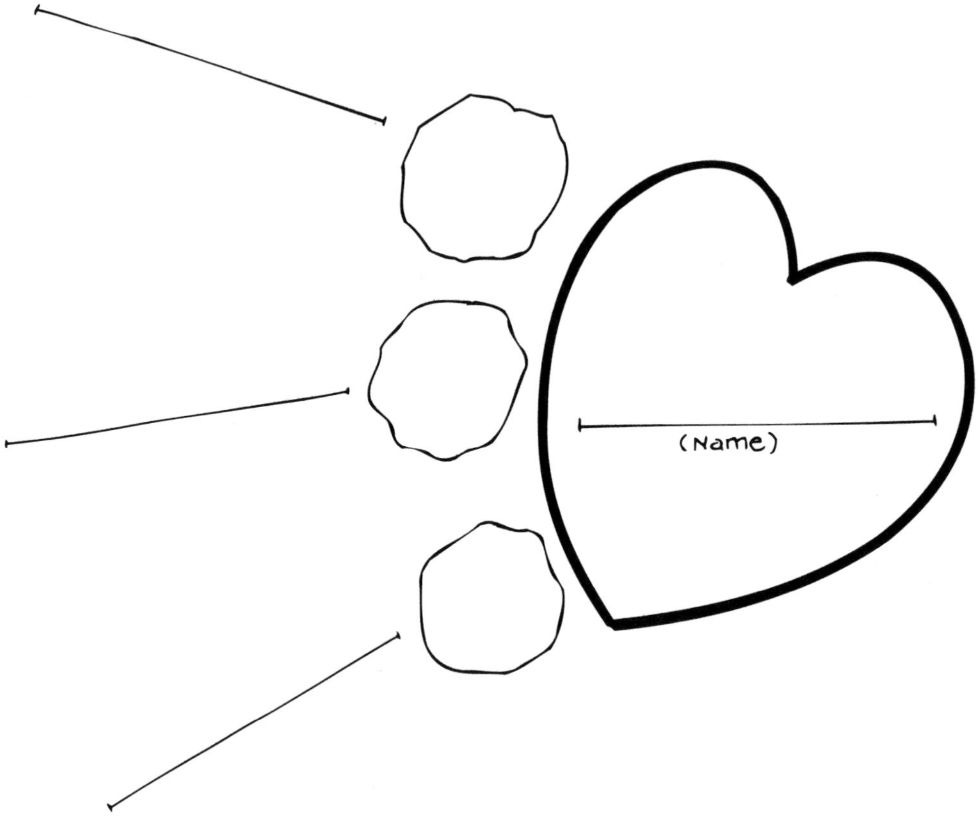

I am convinced that... [nothing] will be able to separate us from the love of God. Romans 8:38-39

Determination!

song

I'm determined!
I'm determined!
I will always do what is right.
I'm determined!
I'm determined!
I will always do what is right.

Spoken: Determination!

I'm determined!
I'm determined!
God's ways are better than my friends'.
I'm determined!
I'm determined!
God's ways are better than my friends'.

Spoken: Determination!

I'm determined!
I'm determined!
I've decided I will stand with God.
I'm determined!
I'm determined!
I've decided I will stand with God.

Spoken: Determination!

Directions

Sing to the tune of "Deep and Wide." Do your students understand the word "determination"? Discuss ways that we can be determined to do what is right, be determined to make decisions based on the Bible rather than what our friends say, and be determined to stand with God. This song is a good review of commitment to be determined! The children will especially enjoy shouting "Determination!" at the end of each verse.

puzzle

Materials

- •puzzle, duplicated
- •pencils

Usage

Distribute this sheet as the students arrive for class. As they figure out the words, they will also be learning the lesson's memory verse. After all have finished, review the verse and discuss its meaning.

My Jewel of Determination

Nothing Between

Don't let anything come between you and living for God!
We kept everything from getting between the verse below, but now we can't find out where to divide the words. Can you help?

IamconvincedthatnothingwillbeabletoseparateusfromtheloveofGod.Romans8:38-39

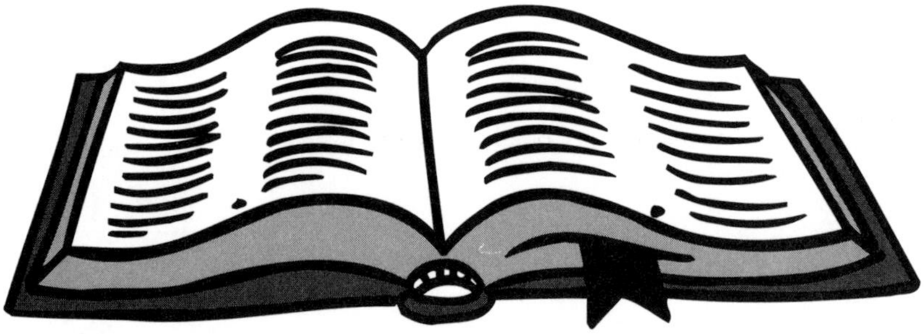

Solution is on page 96.

Soap Crowns

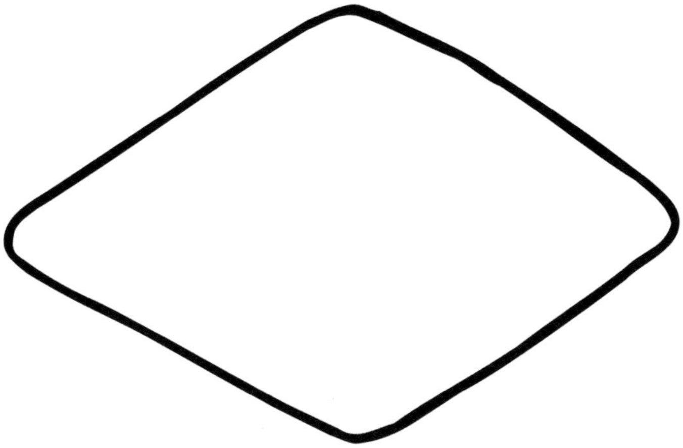

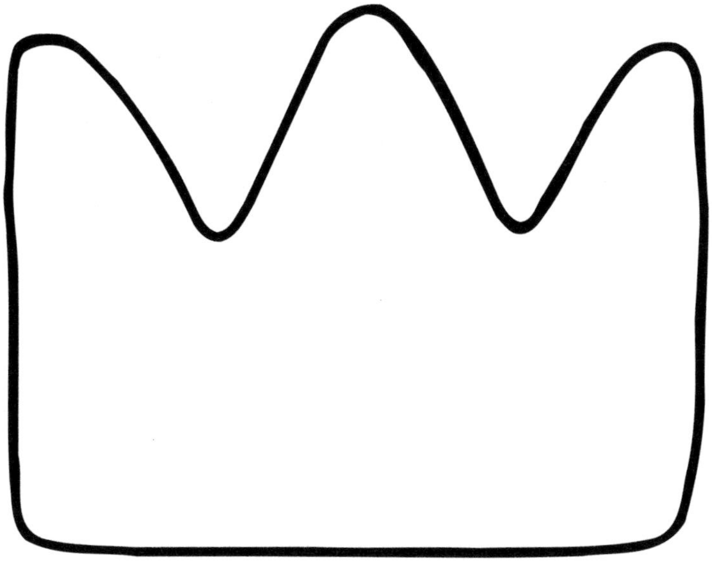

craft

Materials

- patterns, duplicated, or cookie cutters
- 2 cups of soap flakes
- ½ cup of warm water
- food coloring
- waxed paper
- bowl
- egg beater
- measuring cups

Directions

1. Have the students measure the soap and water into a bowl. This recipe may be doubled.
2. Assign someone to stir the mix until the soap dissolves.
3. Add food coloring.
4. Beat the mixture until smooth.
5. Give each child some waxed paper to place on the patterns. Show how to shape the soap to the patterns. Allow 45 minutes to dry before moving.
6. Say, **When you take baths this week, use your soap and say, "Nothing will separate me from the love of God. I have the jewel of determination!"**

My Jewel of Determination

Separation Jump

game

Materials

- 17 small toys and books
- jewel badge, duplicated to bright paper
- scissors
- double-sided tape

Directions

1. Cut out one jewel badge for each student.
2. Place the toys in a continuous line, leaving room for the children to jump over them.
3. Have the students start at one end and jump over each toy, saying a word of the memory verse as they jump.
4. At the end, give them their jewel badge to wear, attaching it with tape. Say, **You did a good job at being determined to jump over the toys! God says we should all be determined to live for Him.**

Smiling Faces

Draw a line from one smiling face to its twin.

When we are determined to live for God, we have joy in our hearts. That's what makes us smile!

Solution is on page 96.

snack/puzzle

Materials

- puzzle, duplicated
- pencils
- powdered sugar
- measuring cup
- water
- plastic knives
- waxed paper
- flat cookies
- chocolate chips
- candy corn
- red licorice

Directions

1. Have the class work on the puzzle as you prepare the snack.
2. Mix ½ cup of powdered sugar with a little water, stirring until the mixture is creamy.
3. Give each child some waxed paper.
4. Show how to spread the sugar glue on a cookie.
5. Allow them to make a face using chocolate chips, candy corn and licorice.

Discuss

Ask, **Why was Stephen happy to help when he was asked to serve? When we are determined to live for God, we have joy in our hearts. That's what makes us smile!**

My Jewel of Determination

God's Determined Man

craft/skit

Materials

- faces, mouth and script, duplicated
- paper lunch sacks
- glue
- scissors
- markers
- two chairs
- large dowel rod or broom handle
- old sheet or fabric
- aluminum foil

Directions

1. Have the class color and cut out the faces and mouths.
2. Show how to glue them to the sacks to make puppets.
3. Place 2 chairs a few feet apart, backs facing each other.
4. Lay the broom handle across the backs of the chairs.
5. Hang the sheet over the chairs and the stick for the stage. Write "A Determined Man" on the sheet.
6. Crumple foil in balls for stones.
7. Read the script and have the children take turns using their puppets to tell the story.

My Jewel of Determination

God's Determined Man

Disciple: Stephen, will you take over the feeding of the widows? We are busy and need your help.

Stephen: Yes. I will be happy to serve in any way I can. *dances back and forth and hums*

High Priest enters. Stephen stands still.

Elders: This man speaks blasphemous words against Moses and God.

High Priest: What? Is this want you have said? Take him out and stone him!

High Priest leaves. Elders begin to throw foil stones.

Stephen: Lord Jesus, forgive these people. *lays on side*

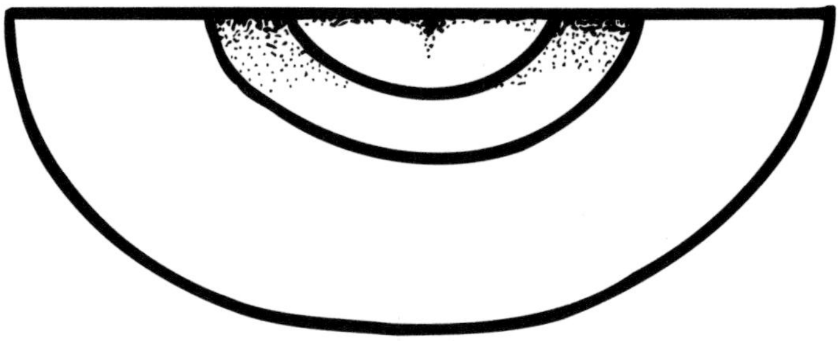

Mouth
(use for all four puppets)

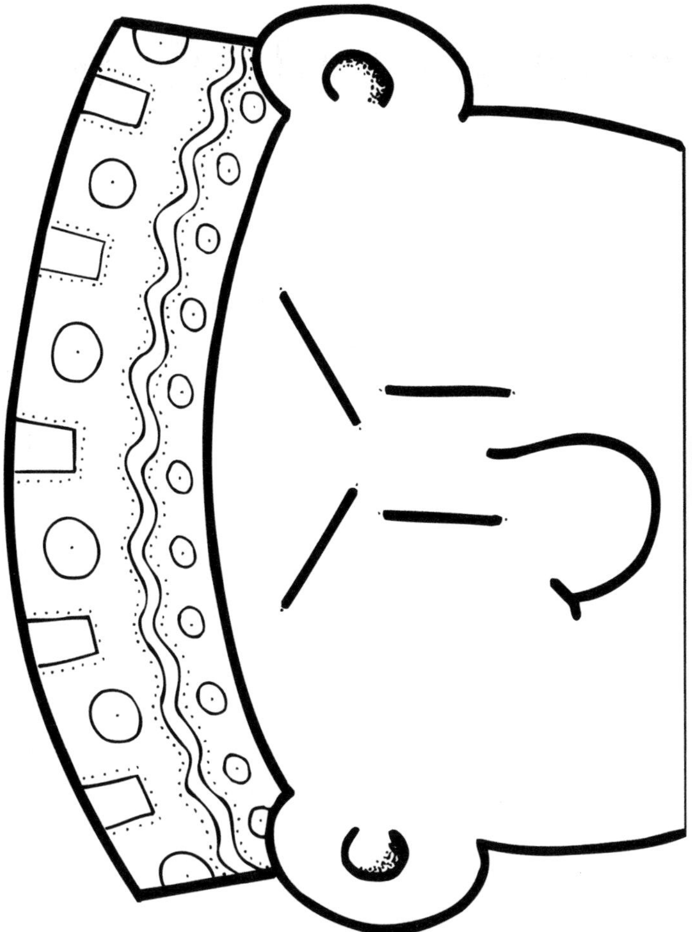
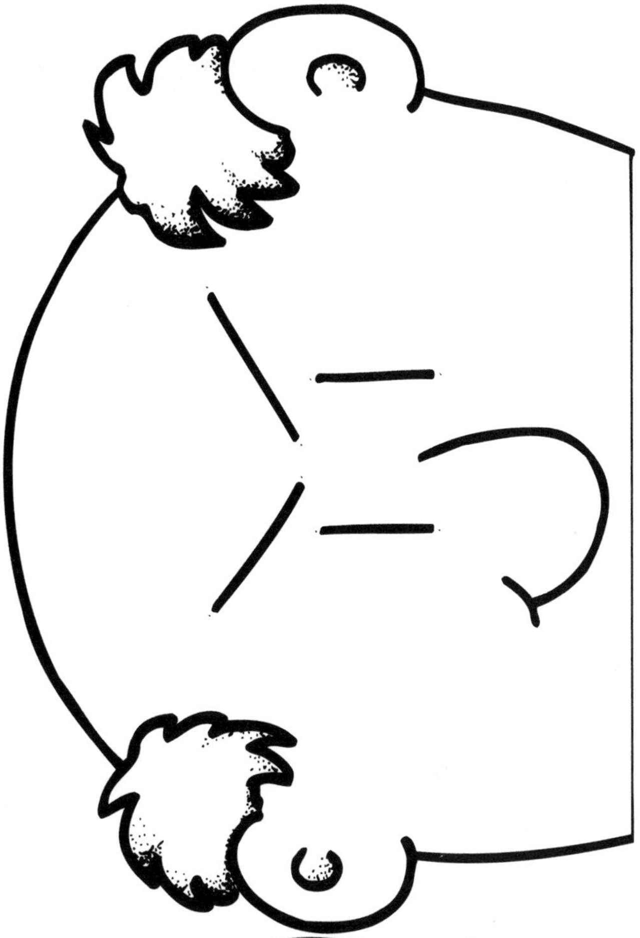

Chapter 6
My Jewel of Appreciation

Memory Verse

Let them sacrifice thank offerings and tell of his works with songs of joy. Psalm 107:22

Story to Share

A Beautiful Expression of Thankfulness

What can I do to show Jesus how much I love Him? Mary asked herself. Mary's heart was overflowing with love for Jesus, who had done so much for her. But her heart was also aching with the desire to let Jesus know the depth of her love for Him.

Jesus was staying at the home of His friends, Mary and Martha, and their brother Lazarus. Some time before, Lazarus had died and they put him in a tomb. Jesus had raised him from the dead.

Mary knew her sister Martha had prepared a special dinner in Jesus' honor. As Martha busied herself serving, Mary once again wondered what she could do to show her great love and appreciation for Him.

Suddenly, she an idea. She didn't care about the cost involved. She picked up her alabaster jar of pure nard, a valuable ointment that came from India. Bending low, Mary broke the long neck of the flask and poured the precious oil on Jesus' feet, rubbing the ointment in, then wiping His feet clean with her hair.

As the whole house was filled with the pure nard's sweet smell, Mary heard the murmur of voices around her.

"Can you believe what she did?" exclaimed one. "What wastefulness!"

"A whole year's wages!" grumbled another. "She should have sold it and given the money to the poor."

Why doesn't anyone understand, Mary thought. She had done this to show her love for Jesus. A tear ran down her cheek. Then she heard Jesus speak.

"Leave her alone," He said gently. "She has done a beautiful thing. You'll always have the poor with you; you can help them whenever you want. But you won't always have Me here with you. This act of love will always be remembered."

A great joy filled Mary's heart. Jesus understood her love and appreciation.

— based on John 12:1-7

Questions for Discussion

1. What are some things you have for which you can thank God?
2. For what can you thank your mother? Your teacher? Your father? Your sister or brother?

craft

Materials

- bottle, duplicated to heavy paper
- scissors
- string or yarn
- hole punch

Directions

1. Cut a length of string for each child.
2. Have the class cut out the bottle and punch holes at the dots.
3. Show the students how to make a cut at each line by the words of the memory verse.
4. Help them thread string through the top hole and knot on the back.
5. Instruct the children to wrap the string from one notch to another, in the order of the memory verse.
6. Have them end at the bottom hole and knot in the back.

My Jewel of Appreciation

Thank Offerings

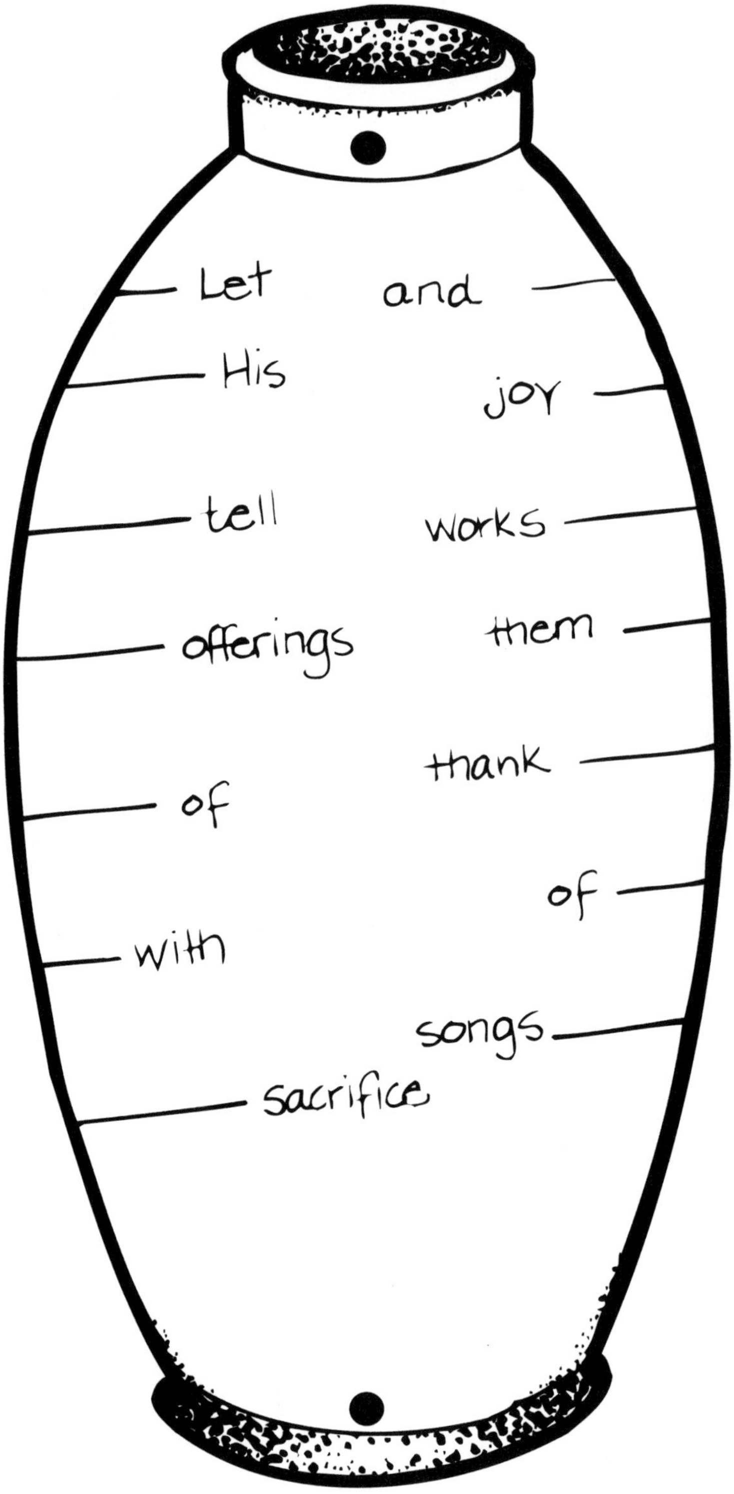

Solution is on page 96.

Appreciation Walkie Talkies

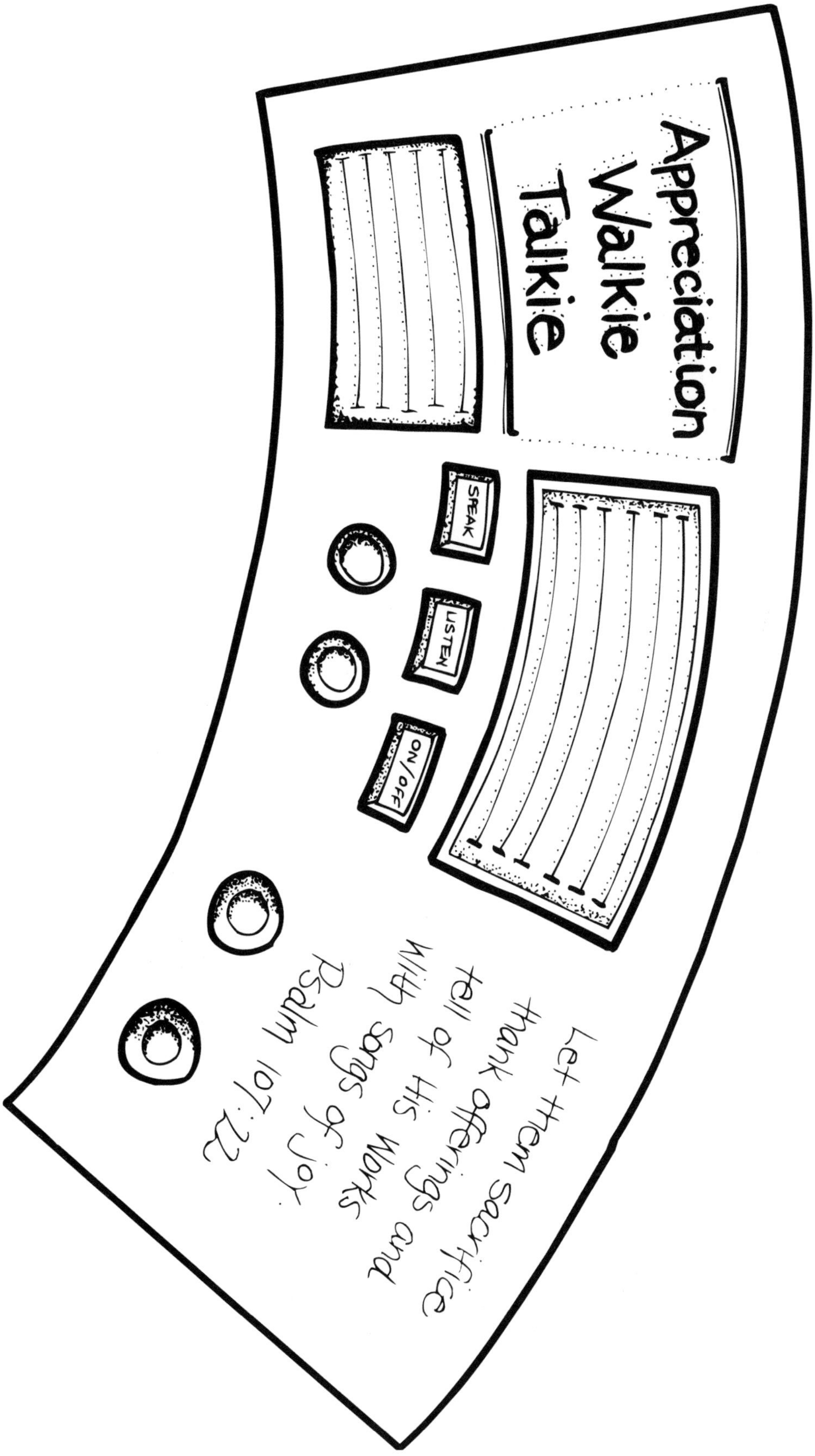
Appreciation
Walkie
Talkie
SPEAK
LISTEN
ON/OFF
Let them sacrifice
thank offerings and
tell of His works
with songs of joy.
Psalm 107:22

activity

Materials

- illustration, duplicated
- paper cups
- string
- scissors
- glue
- pencils

Directions

1. Give each student two cups, six feet of string and two copies of the illustration.
2. Have them use pencils to punch a small hole in the cup bottoms.
3. Allow the students to cut out and glue the illustration on the outside.
4. Help them thread the string through the hole in each cup and knot the ends.
5. Instruct the children to pick a partner and move apart until the string is tight.
6. One partner should put a cup at his ear while the other talks into a cup. Say, **Whisper why you like your partner.**

Discuss

Say, **"Appreciation" means to be thankful for what others do for us. For what can we be thankful to God? Who else can we appreciate?**

My Jewel of Appreciation

song

Directions

Sing to the tune of "Are You Sleeping?" Have each child stand and tell for what they are thankful. Sing the verse with their name in the first two lines and for what they are thankful in the following two. If desired, photocopy the page, then allow the children to fill in the lines and color the pictures of things for which they should be thankful.

I Am Thankful

Let's be thankful.
Let's be thankful.
For God's love.
For God's love.
God takes care of me.
God takes care of you.
Praise the Lord.
Praise the Lord.

__________ is thankful.
__________ is thankful.
For his (her) ______________.
For his (her) ______________.
God takes care of me.
God takes care of you.
Praise the Lord.
Praise the Lord.

My Jewel of Appreciation

Let's Give an Offering

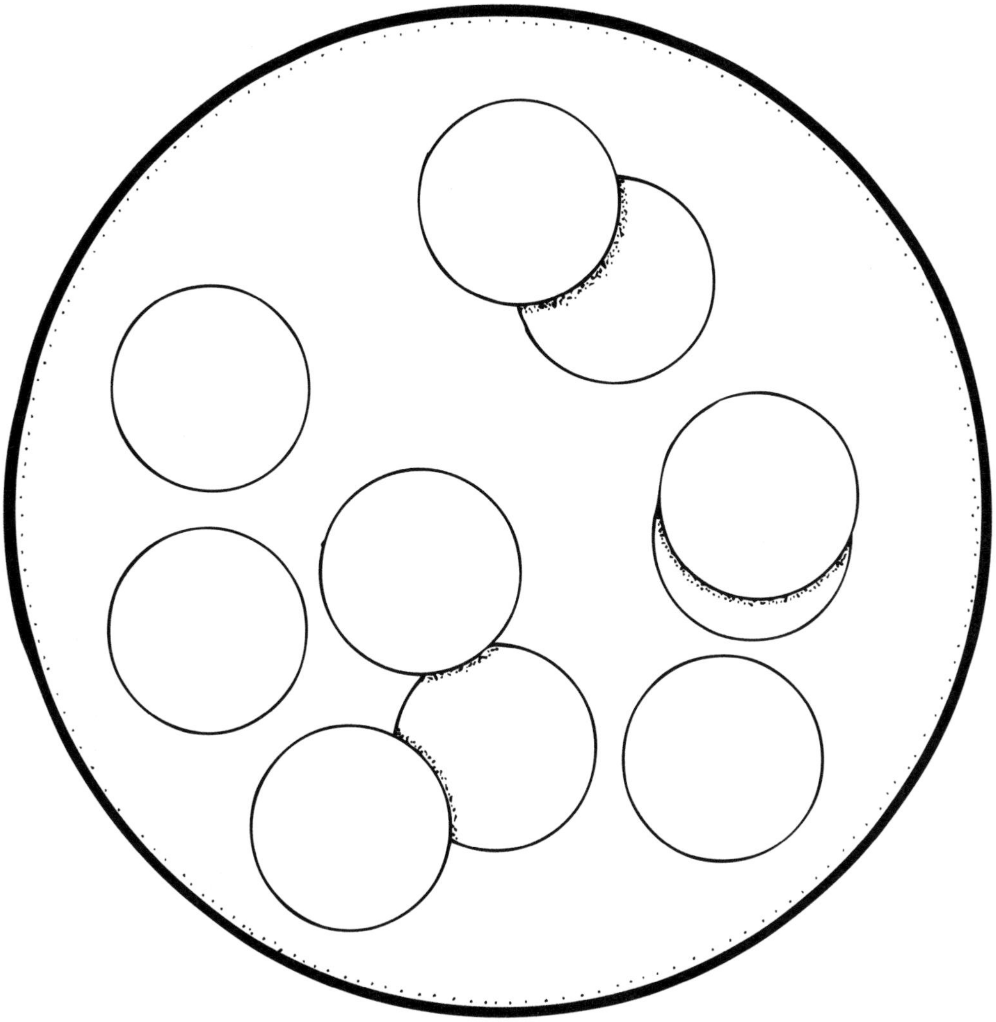

Let them sacrifice thank offerings and tell of his works with songs of joy.
Psalm 107:22

activity

Materials
- offering plate, duplicated
- pencil
- crayons

Directions
1. Instruct the class to write something for which they are thankful on each coin.
2. Allow them to color the offering plate.

Discuss
Ask, **For what do we have to thank God ? What did you eat today? What did you sleep in last night? What are you wearing? Who takes care of you?**

My Jewel of Appreciation

Smiles of Appreciation

snack/song

Materials

- smile and song, duplicated
- red apples, sliced
- peanut butter
- mini marshmallows
- craft sticks
- glue

Directions

1. As you prepare for the snack, have the students color and cut out the smile.
2. They should glue the smile to the top of a craft stick.
3. To make the snack, have the children spread peanut butter on one side of two apple slices.
4. Show them how to place four marshmallows on top of the peanut butter on one slice.
5. Have them top that slice with the other, peanut butter side down, and push down gently to make smiles.
6. After the snack, sing the song to the tune of "Old Mac Donald Had a Farm." The children should hold up their smiles when they spell SMILE.

My Jewel of Appreciation

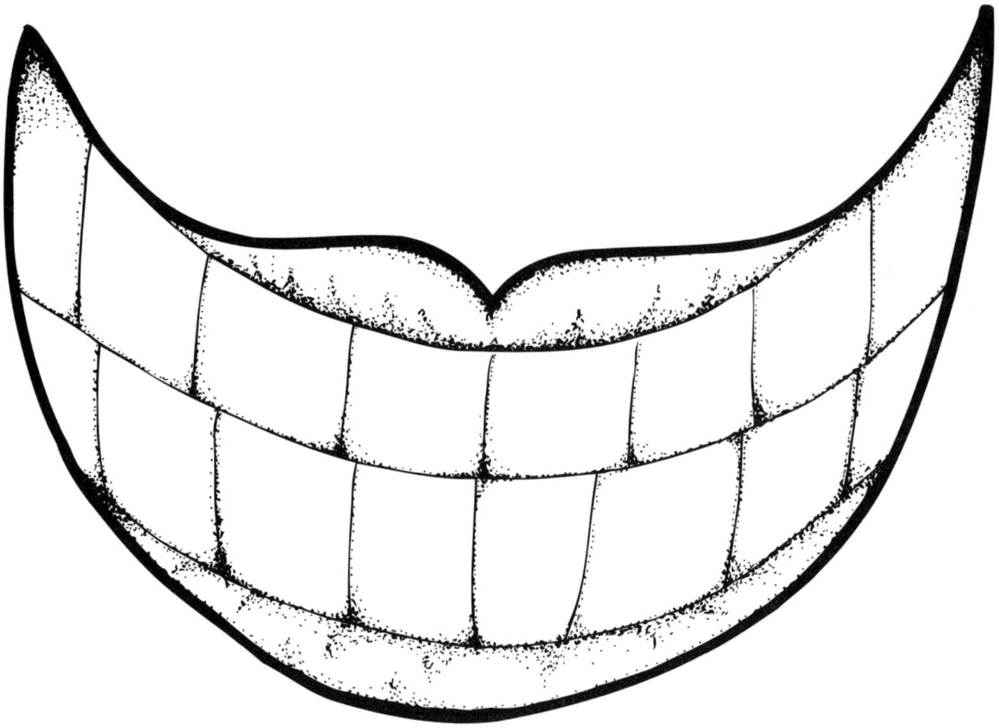

Smile Song

In my heart I have a smile,
S-M-I-L-E.
I like to put it on my face,
S-M-I-L-E.
With a smile here and a smile there.
Here a smile, there a smile;
Saying thank You with my smile.
In my heart I have a smile,
S-M-I-L-E.

Banks of Thanks

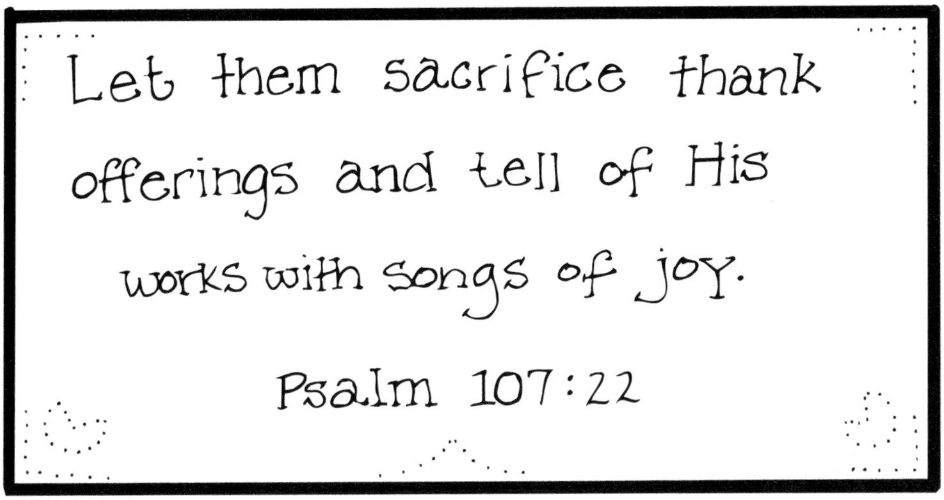
Let them sacrifice thank offerings and tell of His works with songs of joy.
Psalm 107:22

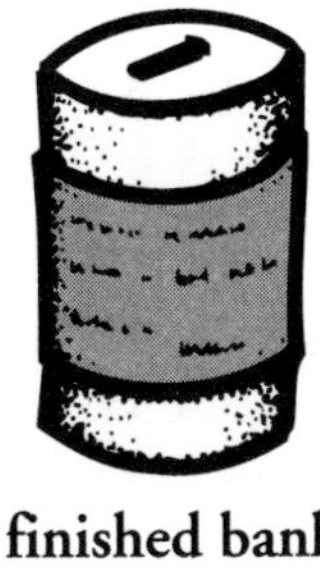

finished bank

craft

Materials

- label, duplicated
- empty containers with lids, small
- markers or crayons
- scissors
- glue
- slips of paper
- pencils

Directions

1. Allow the children to color, cut out and glue the labels to the outside of the containers.
2. Go around the room and cut a slit in the top of each lid.
3. Instruct the class to write what they are thankful for on slips of paper, then place them in their banks.
4. Say, **Each time you think of something for which you are thankful, write it down and make a "deposit" in your bank. Then, when you pray, open up the bank and read your slips to God. It will be a happy "withdrawal" for you and God.**

My Jewel of Appreciation

craft

Dances of Joy

Materials

- puppets, duplicated
- crayons
- scissors
- tape

Directions

1. Have the class color and cut out the puppets.
2. Show how to wrap the puppets around your fingers and tape closed.
3. Say the poem for the class. When you say, "Hallelujah, Praise the Lord!" they should have their finger puppets "dance" in praise.

Hallelujah Poem

Mary loved Jesus.
She told His works with joy.
Hallelujah! Praise the Lord!

I love Jesus.
I tell His works with joy.
Hallelujah! Praise the Lord!

Hallelujah! Praise the Lord!
Hallelujah! Praise the Lord!
I tell His works with joy.

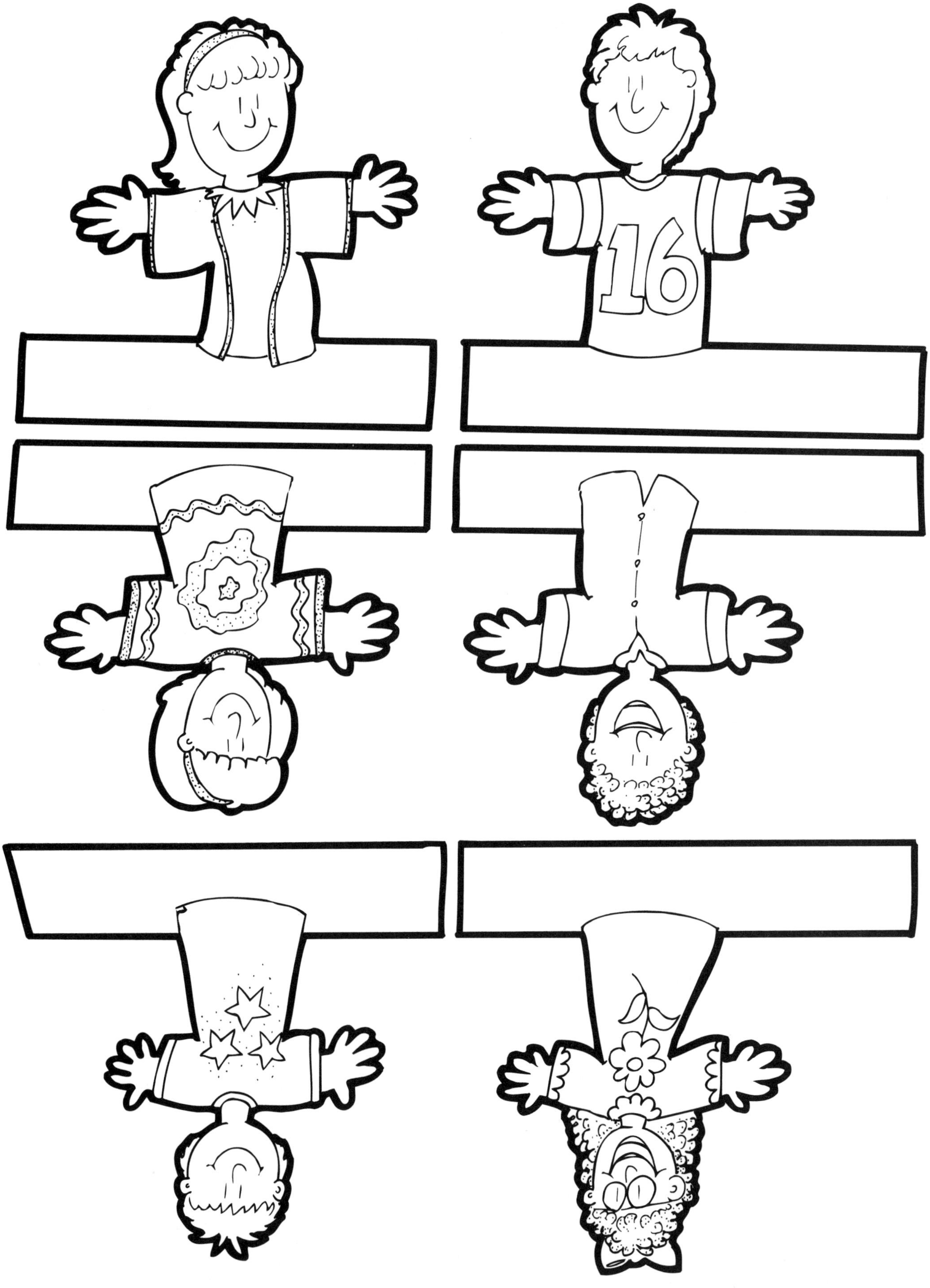
16

Chapter 7
My Jewel of Conviction

Memory Verse

Stand firm in the faith; be men of courage; be strong.
1 Corinthians 16:13

Story to Share

We Stand Firm

Shadrach, Meshach and Abednego were God's faithful servants. They also had important jobs in King Nebuchadnezzar's empire.

One day the king gave an order to build a golden statue of a god and to bow to it.

"We will stand firm to our convictions," Shadrach, Meshach and Abednego pledged together. "Whether we live or die, we will not bow to an idol."

Some of the king's wise men hurried to tell him of this disobedience: "Shadrach, Meshach and Abednego, the three men you chose for important posts in your kingdom, have not bowed down to your god. They disobeyed your orders."

King Nebuchadnezzar flew into a rage. "Bring them to me," he commanded.

"If you do not worship my idol," the king shouted at them, "I will have you thrown into a fiery furnace."

But even in the face of death the three men did not waver in their convictions. "We will not worship your statue," Meshach told the king. "We bow only to the true God."

Their refusal to back down from what they believed angered the king even more. When the three men did not move to bow, the king commanded, "Throw them in the furnace."

The furnace was so hot that the warriors who were ordered to throw them in were killed. Nebuchadnezzar sat back, still angry. Then he quickly jumped to his feet. "Why do I see four men walking free and unharmed in the middle of the flames?" he exclaimed. "The fourth looks like a god."

Then the king called out, "Shadrach, Meshach and Abednego, servants of the most high God, come out!"

Everyone stared in astonishment as the three men walked out of the flames, unburned.

"There is no god greater than the God of these men," said the king. "I decree that anyone who dares to say anything against the God of these men will be cut into pieces and their homes turned into rubble."

Embracing Shadrach, Meshach and Abednego, King Nebuchadnezzar gave them positions of great power in the government of Babylon.

— based on Daniel 3:1-30

Questions for Discussion

1. Would you be frightened if you had to go to the principal's office for not participating in an activity that you know is against God's Word?
2. Would you stand firm to what you know is right?

Who Will Stand Firm?

game

Materials

•badges, duplicated
•tape

Directions

1. Cut out the badges and mix them up.
2. Tape one badge on each child.
3. Have the class sit on the floor.
4. Clap. If you clap once, the 1s stand up and say the memory verse. If you clap twice, the 2s stand up, and so on.
4. Whoever stands up at the wrong time must say the verse alone!
5. When you clap four times, everyone jumps up to quote the verse.

Discuss

Say, **When the king wanted them to bow down to his idol, Shadrach, Meshach and Abednego refused. What are some ways you can stand firm with your friends at school?**

My Jewel of Conviction

Three Didn't Bow

Ten of the king's men all in a line,
One bowed down to the idol and then there were nine.

Nine of the king's men all in a line,
One bowed down to the idol and then there were eight.

Eight of the king's men all in a line,
One bowed down to the idol and then there were seven.

Seven of the king's men all in a line,
One bowed down to the idol and then
there were six.

Six of the king's men all in a line,
One bowed down to the idol and
then there were five.

Five of the king's men all in a line,
One bowed down to the idol and then there were four.

Four of the king's men all in a line,
One bowed down to the idol and then there were three.

Three of the king's men all in a line,
Shadrach, Meshach and Abednego, none would bow down.

Three of the king's men all in a line,
"Into the fiery furnace," the king commanded loudly.

Three of the king's men all in a line,
Plus one other, protecting them in the fire.

Three of the king's men all in a line,
They didn't bow down, they stayed firm.
I want to be a king's man that doesn't bow. YES! YES! YES!

game

Directions

1. Have 10 children stand in a line.
2. As you say the first line at left, the first one in line bows.
3. Continue until three children remain standing.
4. You should join in the line when you say, "Plus one other."
5. Have everyone stand on the last line.

Count Me Out

activity

Materials
- tag, duplicated
- hole punch
- scissors
- yarn
- clear, disposable gloves
- pink jelly beans
- popped popcorn
- twist ties

Directions
1. Give each student a glove and five jelly beans.
2. Have them stuff a jelly bean into each finger of the glove.
3. They may fill the rest of the glove with popcorn.
4. Show how to close the glove with a twist tie.
5. Have them cut out the tag and punch a hole at the dot.
6. Show how to tie the tag onto the hand with a piece of yarn.

Discuss
Say, **Sometimes when you're playing, your friends may want you to do something that will displease Jesus. When that happens, we need to raise our hands and say, "Count me out."**

My Jewel of Conviction

●

Count me out!

Stand firm in the faith; be men of courage; be strong.
1 Corinthians 16:13

finished project

1 Corinthians 16:13 Maze

All of the letters in your memory verse are in the furnace.
Start at the arrow and draw a line from one letter to the next letter
until you find them all. Don't use any letters twice!
Then write the verse on the lines below.

Solution is on page 96.

puzzle

Materials

- puzzle, duplicated
- pencils

Usage

Once the children figure out the first letter of the memory verse, they can make one continuous line to form the whole verse from the puzzle. You may need to assist younger children, possibly asking the class to call out each letter as they draw the line together.

My Jewel of Conviction

craft

Materials

- can wrap, duplicated
- soft drink cans, tabs removed
- dried beans
- measuring spoons
- tape
- crayons or markers

Directions

1. Have the students spoon two tablespoons of dried beans into a can.
2. Show how to tape the opening closed. Caution the children to be extra careful around the sharp edges. For younger children, you may want to tape the opening to avoid cuts.
3. Have the class color and cut out the can wrap. They may wrap and tape it around the can.
4. Say the poem at right, encouraging the class to shake their Conviction Shakers at appropriate times.

My Jewel of Conviction

Conviction Shakers

Shaker Poem

1. Shadrach, Meshach and Abednego,
   Bow down.
   WE WILL NOT! *shake can*

2. If you don't bow,
   Into the fiery furnace you'll go.
   WE WILL NOT! *shake can*

3. Conviction,
   Willing to stand for what I believe.
   YES I WILL! *shake can*

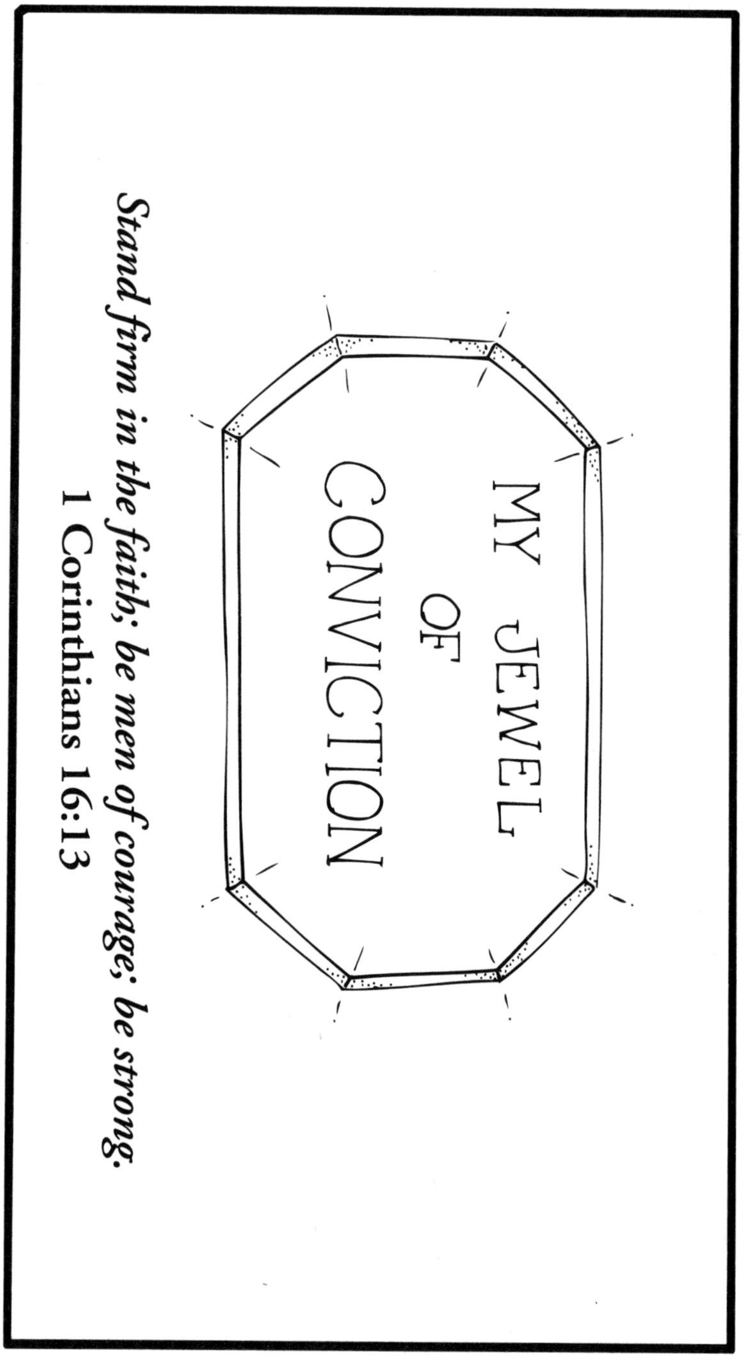

Stand firm in the faith; be men of courage; be strong.
1 Corinthians 16:13
MY JEWEL
OF
CONVICTION

This Is the Way

This is the way we look for Christ, look for Christ, look for Christ.
This is the way we look for Christ,
Every single day. *shade eyes with hand and look up*

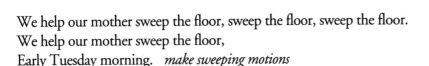

We tell our friends about our Christ, about our Christ, about our Christ.
We tell our friends about our Christ,
Early Monday morning. *turn to friend and shake finger*

We help our mother sweep the floor, sweep the floor, sweep the floor.
We help our mother sweep the floor,
Early Tuesday morning. *make sweeping motions*

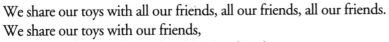

We invite a friend to Sunday School, Sunday School, Sunday School.
We invite a friend to Sunday School,
Early Wednesday morning. *beckon with hand*

We share our toys with all our friends, all our friends, all our friends.
We share our toys with our friends,
Early Thursday morning. *hand "toy" to friend*

We pray for sick and needy friends, needy friends, needy friends.
We pray for sick and needy friends.
Early Friday morning. *fold hands in prayer*

We help our father wash the car, wash the car, wash the car.
We help our father wash the car,
Early Saturday morning. *make circles with hand in air*

This is the way we go to church, go to church, go to church,
This is the way we go to church,
Early Sunday morning. *walk in circle*

Repeat verse one.

song

Directions

Sing to the tune of "This Is The Way We Wash Our Clothes." Teach the class the motions first, then add the song.

You Tell the Story!

craft/skit

Materials

- story figures, duplicated to heavy paper
- script, duplicated
- crayons or markers
- construction paper
- scissors
- clear, self-stick paper

Directions

1. Have the students color and cut out the story figures.
2. Help them to lay the figures on clear, self-stick paper and cover, then cut out again.
3. Encourage the children to use the script as a starting point to tell the story with the figures. They may create their own versions of the story, too.
4. Say, **Take your story figures home and make sure you tell at least one person the story this week.**

Use your story figures to tell about Shadrach, Meshach and Abednego. Here is a script to get you started:

King:	Bow down to my idol.
Shadrach:	I will not!
Meshach:	I will not!
Abednego:	I will not!
King:	Throw them into the furnace.
Shadrach:	I still will not bow!
Meshach:	I still will not bow!
Abednego:	I still will not bow!
King:	Do I see four men? Bring them out!
Shadrach:	I stood firm!
Meshach:	I stood firm!
Abednego:	I stood firm!
King:	Your God is mighty.

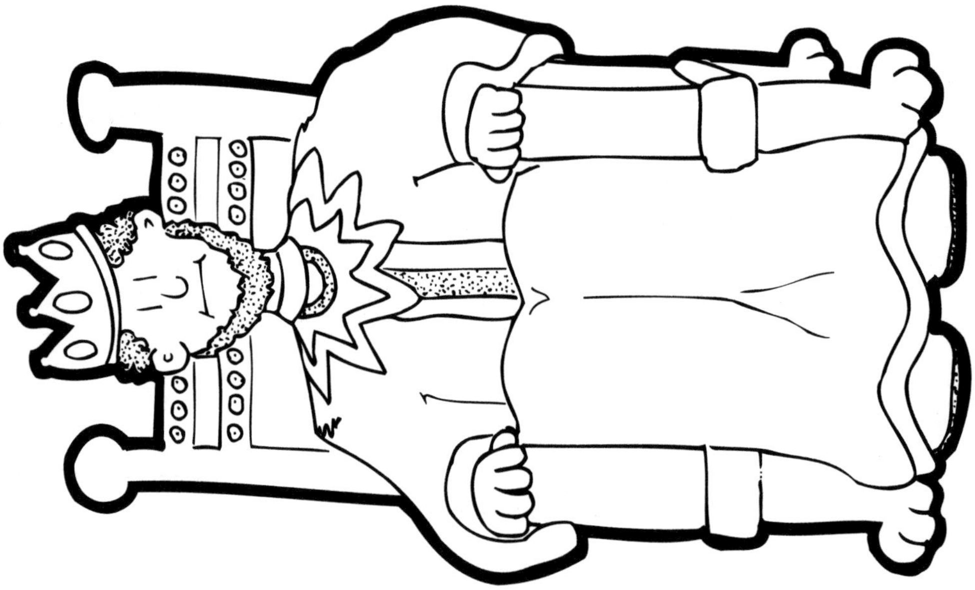

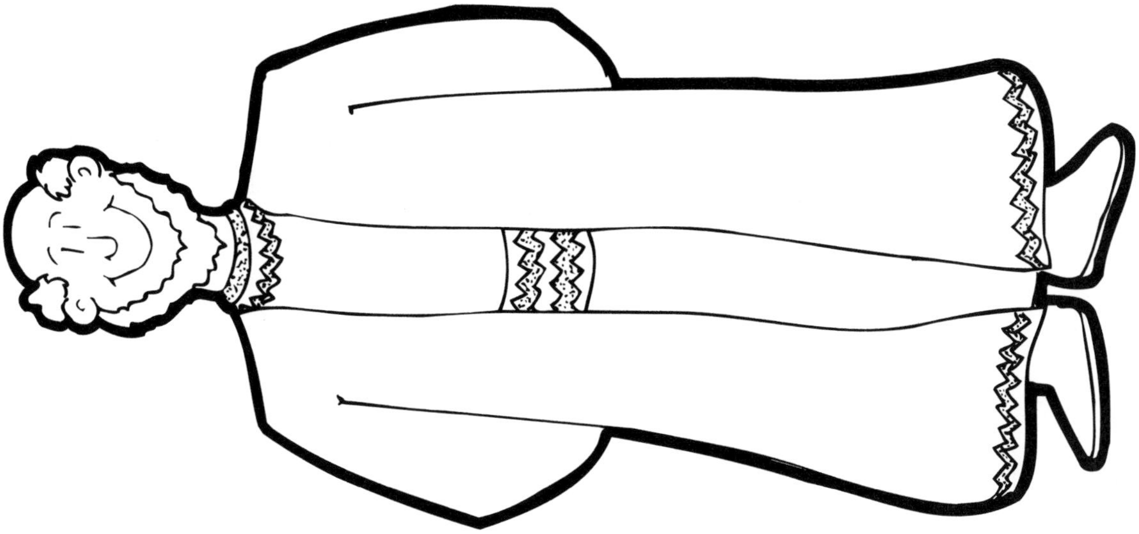

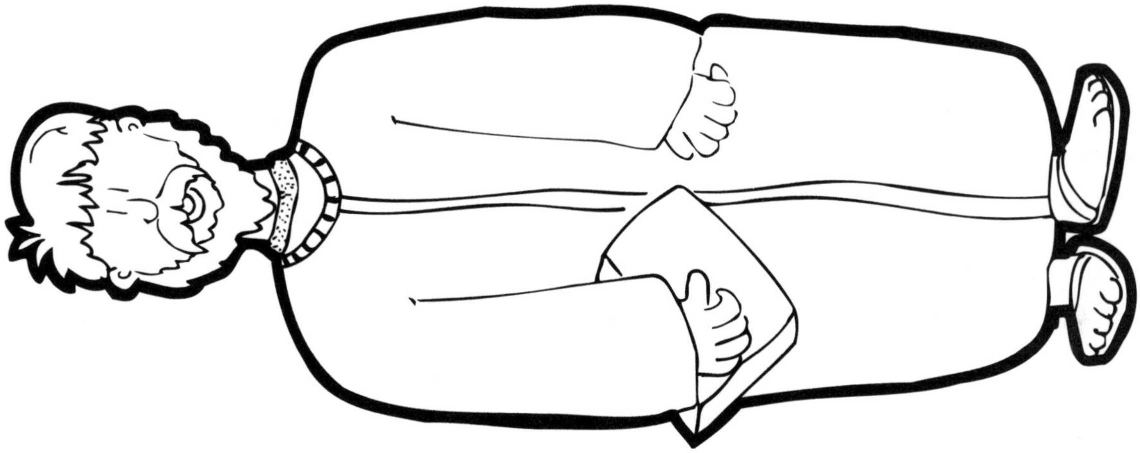

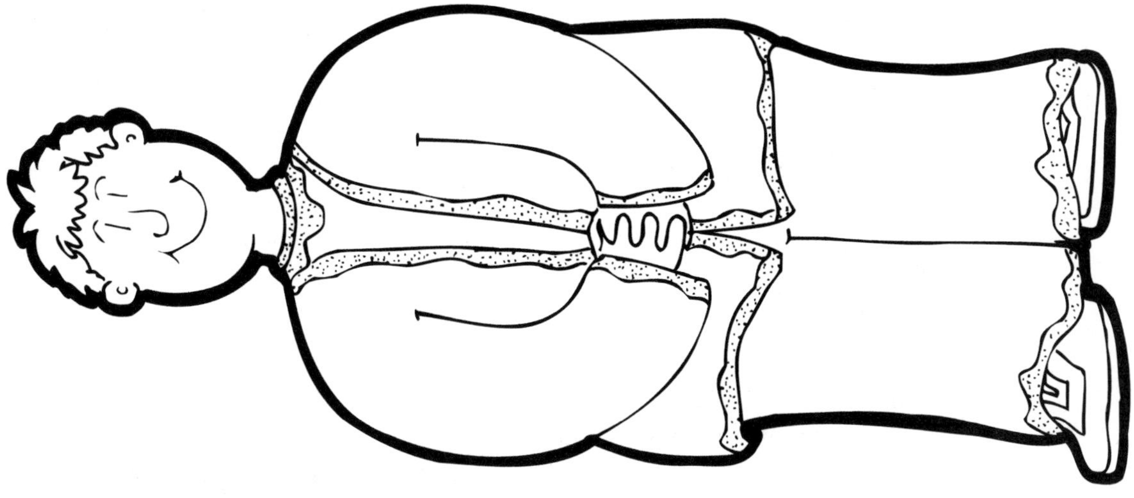

Use Them!

puzzle

Materials

- activity sheet
- crayons

Directions

1. Before class, duplicate the activity sheet for each child.
2. Say, **There is a hidden shape in this picture. It is something that Jesus wants you to use. Color the 's red and the 's blue to see the surprise.**

craft

Handy Reminder

Let not
your hands
be idle
Ecclesiastes 11:6

Materials

- hand pattern
- clear plastic lids
- broken crayons
- tissues
- safety scissors
- glue
- yarn

Directions

1. Before class, duplicate the hand pattern for each child.
2. Show the children how to color the hand pattern, pressing down as firmly as possible with a bright color.
3. Demonstrate how to rub the colored hand with tissues until it is smooth and shiny.
4. Assist in cutting out the hands.
5. Allow the students to glue the hand to the lid.
6. Punch a hole near the top of the lid and tie on a piece of yarn for a hanger.

Let not
your hands
be idle
Ecclesiastes 11:6

My Hands Belong to Jesus

Chapter 8
My Jewel of Adoration

Memory Verse

They lay their crowns before the throne and say: "You are worthy, our Lord and God, to receive glory and honor and power."
Revelation 4:10-11

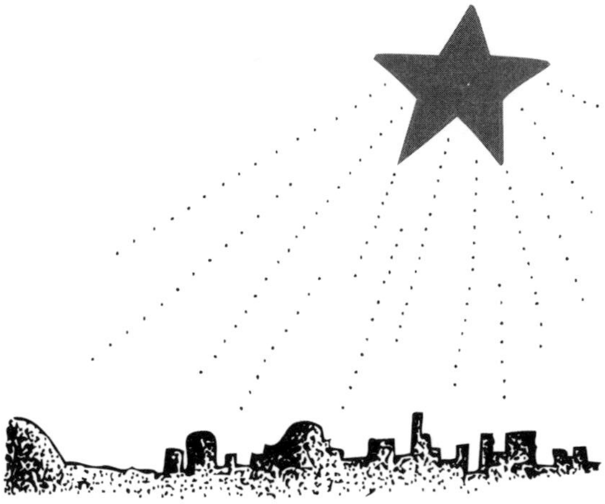

Story to Share

Adoring the Newborn King

The Messiah had been born! The wise men from the East, who were astrologers, were sure of it. "Look at that bright star we can see tonight," said a wise man. "Surely something great has happened."

"Yes," agreed another wise man. "It's the star of the King of the Jews. Let's go worship Him."

The wise men visited King Herod first. "We believe a King of the Jews has been born. Do you know where He is? We have seen His star and have come to worship Him," they told the king.

King Herod had not heard about Jesus' birth. He was not happy to hear that another king had been born. He decided to put this new King to death. Gathering together the religious leaders of the Jewish people, he asked, "Where is the King of the Jews supposed to have been born?"

"In Bethlehem," they answered.

Privately, he called the wise men to him. "Go and worship the child. When you find Him, come back and tell me where I can go and worship this King," he lied.

The wise men went to Bethlehem and were guided by the star to baby Jesus, Mary and Joseph.

They were so glad to find the promised Child! They bowed low and worshipped the baby that was born to be King of the Jews.

One of the wise men gave Jesus a gift of gold. Another brought a jar of myrrh, a very special perfume, which could only be worn by important men. The third wise man presented frankincense to make the air sweet. That night, the wise men were warned in a dream to not tell Herod where Jesus was living, so they took a different route back to their homes.

One day soon, we, too, will be able to worship and adore this same King. We will take off our crowns of righteousness and lay them at His feet. The wise men had their turn to adore Jesus, but our turn is coming.

— based on Matthew 2:1-12

Questions for Discussion

1. What does it mean to adore Jesus?
2. The wise men brought gifts to Jesus; what gifts can we bring to Him?

Follow the Star

craft/game

• • • • • • • • • • • •

Materials

- star, duplicated to heavy paper
- scissors
- string
- hole punch
- dowel rod

Directions

1. Cut out the star and punch a hole at the top.
2. Tie a string through the hole and on the end of a dowel rod.
3. Choose a child to be the leader and to carry the star. The others may form a line behind him.
4. The children follow the leader as he hops, marches, skips, etc.
5. When the leader stops and says, "Stop and adore the King," everyone stops and says the memory verse together.
6. The leader then goes to the back and the next child in line becomes the leader. (You may have to ring a bell for the group to stop.)
7. Allow all of the children to make stars to play the game at home.

My Jewel of Adoration

THEY LAY THEIR CROWNS BEFORE THE THRONE AND SAY: "YOU ARE WORTHY, OUR LORD AND GOD, TO RECEIVE GLORY AND HONOR AND POWER."
REVELATION 4:10-11

Mixed-Up Crowns

Some of the words to the memory verse have been mixed up!
Unscrambled the words and write them in the crowns,
then cut out the crowns and glue them on the correct line.

They ____________ their ___________ before the

____________ and say: "You are

____________, our ____________ and God, to

receive _____________ and honor and

____________. Revelation 4:10-11

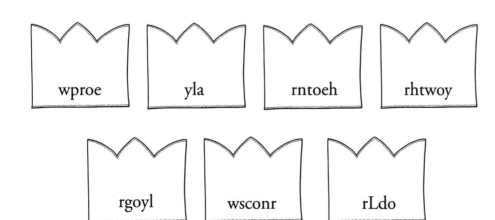

wproe   yla   rntoeh   rhtwoy

rgoyl   wsconr   rLdo

Solution is on page 96.

puzzle

Materials

- •puzzle, duplicated
- •scissors
- •glue

Directions

1. Have the students cut out and glue on the crowns where they belong in the memory verse.
2. Read the verse together when everyone has finished.

craft

A Gift for Jesus

Materials

•illustration, duplicated
•construction paper, various colors
•pencils
•small boxes
•scissors
•glue
•crayons or markers
•bows or ribbon

Directions

1. Show the children how to trace the sides of the box onto construction paper and cut them out.
2. Have them do one of the following to each piece:
   • Write three names for Jesus.
   • Write three words that describe Jesus.
   • Write a sentence on how they feel about Jesus.
   • Cut out, color and glue on the illustration at right.
   • Leave the top and bottom pieces blank.
3. Instruct the children to glue the rectangles where they belong on the box. Let them select a ribbon to glue on the box.
4. Display the boxes or allow the children to use them as gifts.

Discuss

Say, **Just like the Wise Men brought gifts to Jesus, we can make pretend gifts that show how we feel about Him. Jesus likes for us to show Him our love and adoration. This gift box will help us to tell Him how we feel.**

Cinnamon Stars

craft

Materials

- •star, duplicated or star cookie cutter
- •1 cup of cinnamon
- •8 T. of apple sauce
- •mixing bowl, spoon
- •rolling pins
- •waxed paper
- •plastic knives
- •toothpicks
- •narrow ribbon

Directions

1. Mix cinnamon and apple sauce, adding more cinnamon to create dough.
2. Give the students some waxed paper and dough.
3. Show them how to roll it out until it is ¼" thick.
4. Have them cut out the star and use it as a pattern to cut the shape from the dough.
5. Instruct them to poke a small hole at the top of the star with a toothpick.
6. Allow the stars to dry or microwave them for 1 minute. Turn and cook for :30 more.
7. Cut ribbon for each child and have them thread it through the hole and tie with a bow.

I Will Bow

song

Directions

Sing to the tune of "Old McDonald Had a Farm." If desired, duplicate the page and allow the class to color the illustration and take the sheet home.

**We will bow at Jesus' feet.
When He comes again.
We will bow at Jesus' feet.
When He comes again.**

**With a jewel here,
And a jewel there,
Adoration jewels,
Everywhere.
We'll lay our crown at Jesus' feet.
When He comes again.**

My Jewel of Adoration

The Wise Men's Star

Step 1

Fold the paper in half from the top.

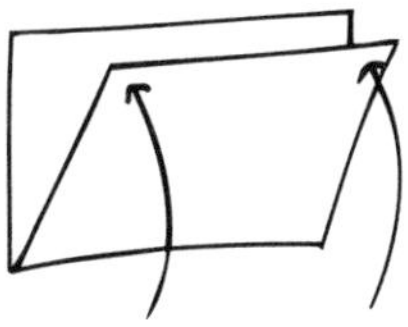

Step 2

With the fold at the bottom, bring the lower right corner up to the halfway point on the left side, and crease.

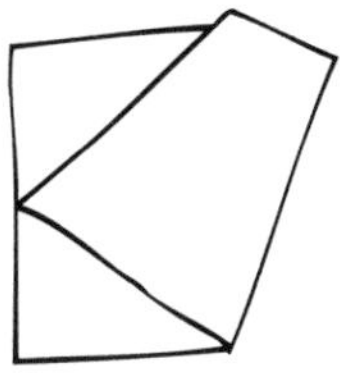

Step 3

Fold the right-hand edge diagonally down to the left to meet the side you brought over in Step 2, and crease.

Step 4

Fold the last section on the left over to the right and crease.

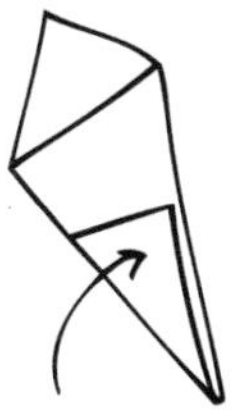

Step 5

Cut at a sharp diagonal line, as shown. The bottom portion is the star.

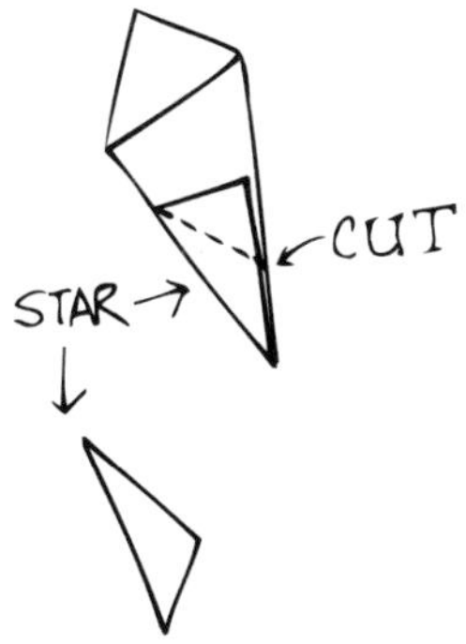

teacher help

Materials

- 8½" x 11" yellow paper
- scissors

Directions

Use this as an object lesson as you tell the story of the wise men's visit to Jesus. Practice the steps first as shown.

Variation

Give each child a piece of paper and show them how to make their own star. For younger children, have the paper already folded with the cut line drawn. Use white paper so they can color it.

Lost Stars

craft

Materials

- •stars, duplicated
- •four box lids, all the same size
- •one box
- •red, blue, green and yellow markers
- •one sheet each of red, blue, green and yellow paper
- •drinking straws
- •scissors
- •glue

Directions

1. Glue the box lids together in a square.
2. Draw a different color of star in the bottom of each lid.
3. Cut 10 stars out of each color of paper.
4. Scatter the stars in the box to mix.
5. Assign one color to each of four children. Have them suck on a straw to pick up the right stars from the box and place them in the lids. The first one to finish says, "I found the star."

Adoration Action

action rhyme/song

Put a crown, put a crown
Put a crown upon my head.
Bright and shining, bright and shining,
Shining crown upon my head.

raise arms as high as possible,
bringing them down to head

Bowing low, bowing low,
Bowing low before my Lord.
I will worship, I will worship,
Bowing low before my Lord.

kneel and place head on floor

He is worthy, He is worthy,
He is worthy of my love.
I will praise Him, I will praise Him,
He is worthy of my love.

hold arms straight out at sides,
then hug self

Directions

You may lead this activity as an action rhyme or it may be sung to the tune of "My Darling Clementine."

Chapter 9
Miscellaneous Jeweled Activities

What a Jewel You Have!

Dear Parent:

Thank you for allowing ____________________ to join us in studying about our CROWN OF RIGHTEOUSNESS. This is what we have been doing in class:

____

____

____

____

Thank you!

____
(teacher)

They shall be mine...in the day I make up my treasured possession. Malachi 3:17

teacher help

Directions

Duplicate and distribute the note. Check off the items you need and insert the date on the blank line when you want them brought in. You may issue one note at the beginning of the eight lessons or issue one note per week or every few weeks, depending on your needs.

Help!

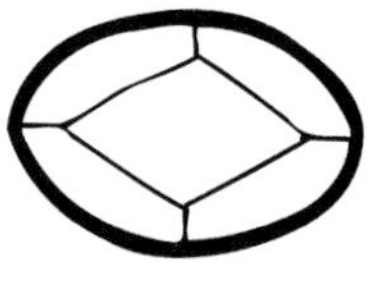

Dear Parents and Friends,

We are learning about the crown of righteousness. There are some "jewels" we need for upcoming lessons on the virtues and values in our crowns. Could you help by sending the following items by ______________________?

- ❑ almonds, sliced
- ❑ aluminum foil
- ❑ apple sauce
- ❑ apples, red
- ❑ beans, dried
- ❑ cans, soft drink size
- ❑ candy corn
- ❑ cellophane paper, colored
- ❑ cheddar cheese, spray
- ❑ chocolate chips
- ❑ cinnamon
- ❑ cocoa powder
- ❑ containers with lids, small
- ❑ cookies, flat
- ❑ cotton balls
- ❑ craft sticks
- ❑ cups, foam
- ❑ egg beaters
- ❑ faux jewels or beads
- ❑ food coloring
- ❑ gelatin, flavored
- ❑ gloves, clear disposable
- ❑ grocery bags, paper
- ❑ honey
- ❑ jelly beans, pink
- ❑ licorice, red
- ❑ lunch sacks, paper
- ❑ marshmallows, large
- ❑ marshmallows, miniature
- ❑ measuring cups & spoons
- ❑ milk, non-fat powdered
- ❑ paint brushes, new
- ❑ paper cups, small
- ❑ paper plates
- ❑ peanut butter
- ❑ plastic knives
- ❑ plastic drinking straws
- ❑ popped popcorn
- ❑ powdered sugar
- ❑ ribbon
- ❑ rolling pins
- ❑ self-stick plastic, clear
- ❑ sesame seeds
- ❑ soap flakes
- ❑ string
- ❑ swiss cheese slices, wrapped
- ❑ toothpicks
- ❑ twist ties
- ❑ waxed paper
- ❑ yarn

Thanks. You're a real gem!

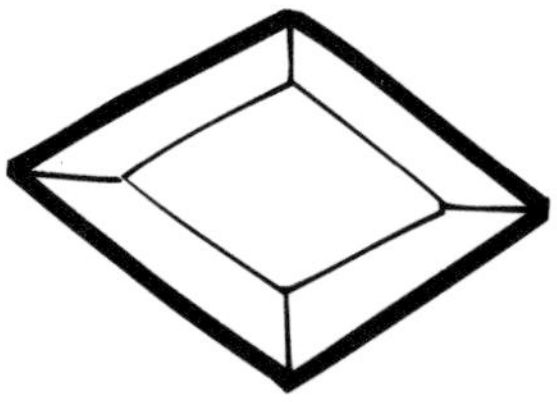

____

(teacher)

Cheese Crowns

Thank You, Jesus, for this food.
You are so very kind and good.
I'll keep my jewels shining bright;
Doing what You say is right.

craft/snack

Materials

- crown, duplicated
- yellow poster board
- colored paper
- scissors
- hole punch
- glue
- clear, self-stick paper
- individually wrapped swiss cheese slices
- spray cheddar cheese

Directions

1. Have the students cut out the large crown and trace it on poster board.
2. They should cut out the poster board crown, then cut the small crown from the pattern.
3. Have them glue it in the center of the large crown.
4. Allow the children to use the hole punch and colored paper to decorate the crowns.
5. Help them cover the crowns with the self-stick paper.
6. To make the snack, cut a crown shape through the middle of the cheese.
7. Show how to make jewels on the crown with the spray cheese. Serve on the crown placemats.

Crown Silhouettes

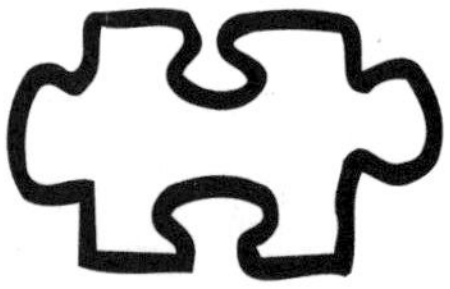

puzzle

Materials

- •puzzle, duplicated
- •pencils

Usage

This puzzle is especially good for the final lesson as a review of the topics discussed in this book. But you may also use it at any time throughout the 8-week session to review and preview lesson themes.

Look at the numbered jewel shapes.
Then look at the jewel pictures in the crown.
Write the name of the jewel on the correct numbered line.

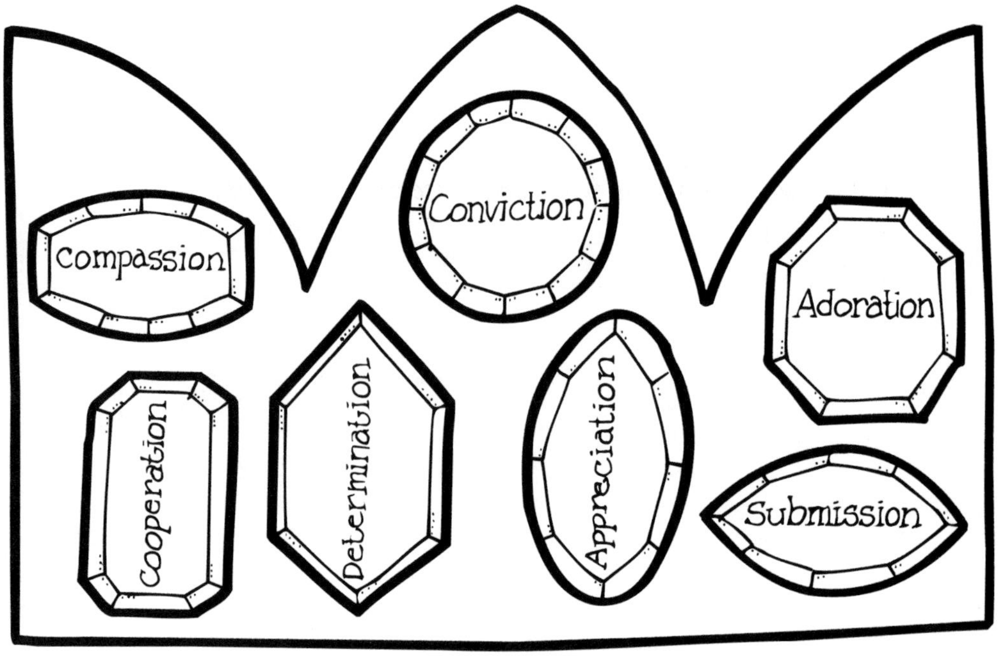

1. ______________________________
2. ______________________________
3. ______________________________
4. ______________________________
5. ______________________________
6. ______________________________
7. ______________________________

Solution is on page 96.

God Is Calling

name, name, God is calling.
He wants you to live for Him.
Will you answer, "Here I am, Lord,"
And offer up your life to Him?

Continue singing the first verse, inserting each pupil's name. As his or her verse is sung, have that child stand up and sing the second verse along with you.

I will, I will, I will answer.
I do want to live for God.
I will answer, "Here I am, Lord,"
And offer up my life to Him.

song

Directions

Sing to the tune of "My Darling Clementine." Your younger students will enjoy having their names added in on the first line.

activity

Kingly Picture

Draw a picture of something you can do to receive your crown of righteousness.

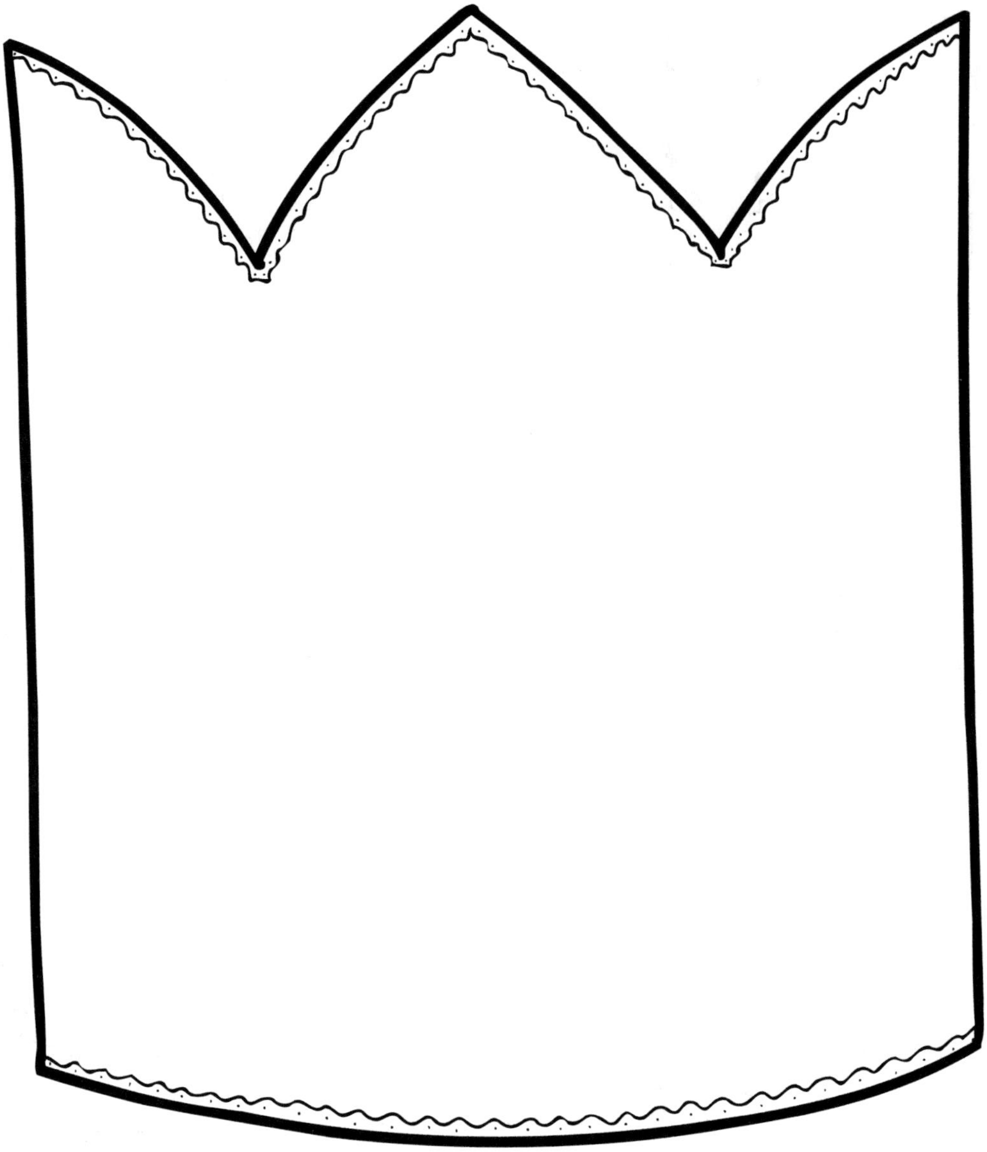

Materials

- crown, duplicated
- pencils
- crayons or markers

Usage

Have this sheet copied and ready for anytime you need a quick filler or a silent activity to quiet your class. You may need to review some possibilities for the illustrations — such as being cooperative, showing compassion, offering appreciation, etc. However, allow the students to draw any godly behavior that may occur to them. Display the finished work on your classroom bulletin board, wall or door with lettering that says "God Gives Me a Crown."

Miscellaneous Jewels

Memory Crowns

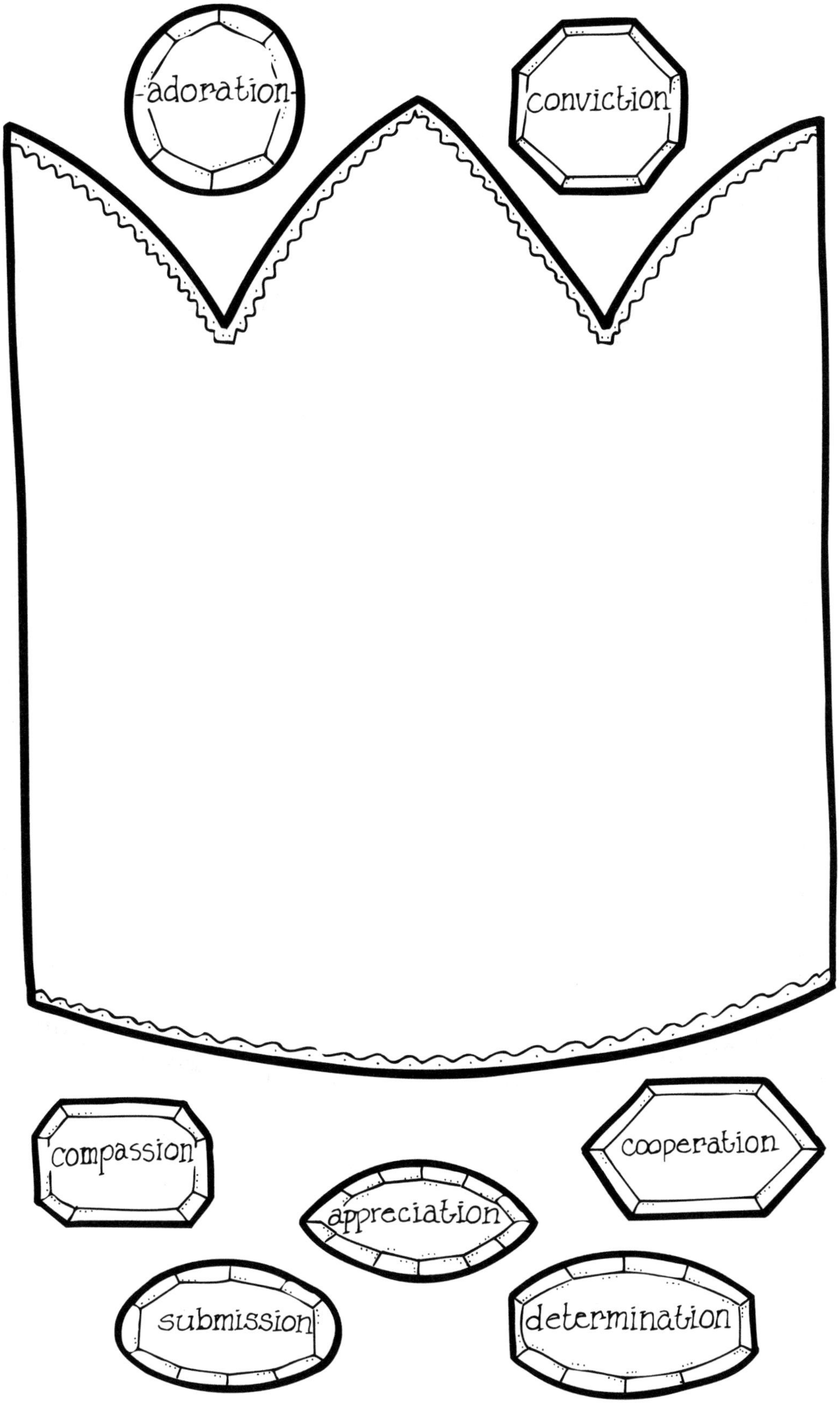

teacher help

Materials

- crown and jewels, duplicated
- fruit-flavored gelatin
- hot water
- paint brush

Directions

1. Cut out a crown and set of jewels for each child. Write their names on the crowns.
2. Pour hot water over the gelatin and mix until dissolved.
3. While the "glue" is still warm, paint it on the backs of the jewels. Allow a few minutes for them to dry.
4. As each memory verse is quoted, have the students lick the coordinating jewel and stick it on the crown.

Variation

Have the children make and update their own Memory Crowns.

I Have My Crown!

game

Materials

- game board and game pieces, duplicated to heavy paper
- penny

Directions

1. After copying, cut out the game pieces at left and fold them on the dashed line so they stand.
2. Give each child a game piece. Split the children into groups of three.
3. Have them toss the penny. Heads equals two spaces, while tails equals one space.
4. They should do whatever the space instructs. If they land on a picture, they must wait until the next turn to move again.
5. Say, **Keep playing until you get that crown!**

START
You're on Your Way!
Slept through Pastor's Sermon -1
Got your Jewel of Compassion +3
Forgot Your Bible -2
Got Your Jewel of Cooperation +3
Got your Jewel of Submission +3
Complained about Weather -2
Got your Jewel of Appreciation +3
Tripped your Neighbor -3
Got your Jewel of Determination +3
BIBLE
Unkind to Teacher -1
Got Your Jewel of Conviction +3
Got Your Jewel of Adoration +3
Disrupted Class -5
Almost there!
You Received Your Crown of Righteousness!!

Answers to Puzzles

Presenting Myself to God, page 10
ME

Stand on Your Head, page 19
His compassions never fail. They are new every morning; great is your faithfulness.
— Lamentations 3:22-23

Compassion, page 24
His compassions never fail. They are new every morning; great is your faithfulness.
— Lamentations 3:22-23; compassion

Here I Come! page 25
His compassions never fail. They are new every morning; great is your faithfulness.
— Lamentations 3:22-23

Add and Solve, page 33
The Lord is my helper; I will not be afraid. — Hebrews 13:6

Jewels of Submission, page 41
men, submissive, those, older, Peter

Nothing Between, page 50
I am convinced that nothing will separate us from the love of God. Romans 8:38-39

Smiling Faces, page 53
Pairs: 1, 9; 2, 10; 3, 8; 4, 6; 5, 12; 7, 11.

Thank Offerings, page 58
Let them sacrifice thank offerings and tell of his works with songs of joy. Psalm 107:22

1 Corinthians 16:13 Maze, page 71

Crown Silhouettes, page 90
1. conviction
2. compassion
3. determination
4. cooperation
5. adoration
6. submission

Mixed Up Crowns, page 79
lay, crowns, throne, worthy, Lord, glory, power